Fashi
or,
Life in New York

A Comedy in Five Acts

by Anna Cora Mowatt

As Devised and Staged
at the Yale Drama School
by Curtis Canfield

A SAMUEL FRENCH ACTING EDITION

SAMUEL FRENCH
FOUNDED 1830

SAMUELFRENCH.COM

DRAMATIS PERSONAE

ADAM TRUEMAN, *a Farmer from Cattcraugus.*
COUNT JOLIMAITRE, *a fashionable European Importation.*
COLONEL HOWARD, *an Officer in the U. S. Army.*
MR. ANTONY TIFFANY, *a New York Merchant.*
T. TENNYSON TWINKLE, *a Modern Poet.*
AUGUSTUS FOGG, *a Drawing Room Appendage.*
JOSEPH SNOBSON, *a rare species of Confidential Clerk.*
ZEKE, *a colored Servant.*
MRS. TIFFANY, *a Lady who imagines herself fashionable.*
PRUDENCE, *a Maiden Lady of a certain age.*
MILLINETTE, *a French Lady's Maid.*
GERTRUDE, *a Governess.*
SERAPHINA TIFFANY, *a Belle.*
TWO FASHIONABLE LADIES, *guests at the Ball.*

SCENES

ACT ONE—*A splendid Drawing Room in the House of* MRS. TIFFANY.
ACT TWO
    SCENE 1. *Inner apartment of* MR. TIFFANY'S *Counting House.*
    SCENE 2. *The Interior of a Beautiful Conservatory.*
ACT THREE
    SCENE 1. *The Splendid Drawing Room.*
    SCENE 2. *The Housekeeper's Room.*
ACT FOUR
    SCENE 1. *An Elegant Ballroom in the House of* MRS. TIFFANY.
    SCENE 2. *The Housekeeper's Room.*
ACT FIVE—*The Splendid Drawing Room.*
    (It is suggested that there be one intermission between Acts Three and Four.)

MUSICAL SELECTIONS

The words and accompanying stage business for them are included in this text. Copies of the Piano score containing the melodies for these, with an Overture and incidental music by Richmond Browne, may be obtained from Samuel French, Inc.

Four of the songs, according to Sigmund Spaeth in his memorable collection, *Read 'Em And Weep,* were used by Brian Hooker in the Provincetown Playhouse production of *Fashion* in the Twenties. These were *Not For Joe, Walking Down Broadway, Call Me Pet Names,* and *Croquet.* To these have been added the remainder which also seemed to be in keeping with the spirit of the comedy. The complete list follows:

Walking Down Broadway . . . . COUNT, SERAPHINA, MRS. TIFFANY

Not For Joe . . . . MR. SNOBSON

Camptown Races . . . . ZEKE

Call Me Pet Names . . . . . COLONEL HOWARD, GERTRUDE

Croquet . . . . MR. TWINKLE

I Wish I Was Single Again . . . . MR. TIFFANY

The Gypsy's Warning . . . . MILLINETTE

The Man Who Broke the Bank at Monte Carlo . . COUNT

Why Did They Dig Ma's Grave So Deep?
> Ensemble: MRS. TIFFANY, MR. TWINKLE, SERAPHINA, MILLINETTE, HOWARD, MR. FOGG, MR. SNOBSON.

She's Only a Bird in a Gilded Cage
> MR. TRUEMAN and Ensemble: COUNT, MR. SNOBSON, MR. TIFFANY, MR. TWINKLE, MR. FOGG, COL. HOWARD, GERTRUDE.*

* The choral numbers may be divided among the members of the cast in accordance with the quality of the voices. When casting, the singing abilities of the various characters must be considered.

4

NOTES ON THE PRODUCTION

This production should be staged as if the entertainment were being presented by a traveling stock company in the 1880's or '90's. The costumes should be designed accordingly. The sets should consist of painted theatrical drops and permanent wings, with a limited amount of furniture. If the drops can combine both a certain naïveté and sophistication, so much the better.

In no case should the roles be hammed. Mrs. Mowatt, although she wrote the play more than a hundred years ago for an audience less used to realism than today's, meant the asides and some of the straight matter to be funny; but she probably meant the play's sentiments to be taken seriously. Although this latter may be somewhat hard to do now, the more serious Mr. Trueman is about his country ideals and his patriotic feelings, and the more formal and idealistic Colonel Howard and Gertrude are in their attitudes, the better. Their postures, though somewhat mannered, should not be carried to the point of caricature. The material should be approached with gentle humor and without condescension, although at times it may be legitimate to let Mr. Snobson, for instance, assume truly villainous proportions and Mr. Tiffany rather extreme postures of repentance and despair.

Count Jolimaitre must be played with zest. His peccadilloes should have an engaging quality in keeping with his eventual reformation. In no way should he echo the darker-colored villainy of Mr. Snobson. He should speak with an Oxford accent with occasional lapses into Cockney.

Colonel Howard is the essence of punctilio with a kind of humorless formality which is best expressed by a deadpan facial mask and utter economy in moves and gestures. He should, of course, be handsome in accord-

5

ance with the matinee-idol ideal, and unbending in bearing.

Mr. Tiffany is small in stature, "little Antony," and most frequently wears a resigned if not apprehensive expression. When he does revolt against his wife's extravagances, he should show that he knows he is fighting a losing battle. He must make the most of the chances which his solo, "I Wish I Was Single Again," gives him to convey his true feelings.

Mr. Twinkle is affected but not effeminate. A flowing tie is enough to suggest his poetic inclinations.

Zeke describes Mr. Fogg as a "bery misty-looking gemman" which gives the director latitude in determining how he shall be played. At Yale we threw a cloak around his shoulders and played him as a sort of statuesque Shakespearean actor, very pale of countenance and, of course, very bored.

Circumstances should dictate the length to which Snobson should carry out the role of the conventional villain of melodrama. An occasional satanic laugh or threatening gesture toward the audience fixes the role. He must play with considerable energy and it should be made clear, in costume as well as speech, that he moves in a much lower social order than those who are welcomed to Mrs. Tiffany's house.

Zeke should be conventionalized in burnt-cork make-up but without recourse to any other minstrel-show exaggerations. Mrs. Mowatt did not have a good ear for Negro dialect and perhaps this deficiency may be corrected. Symbolically associated with his mistress, Mrs. Tiffany, in their mutual difficulties with language, Zeke should be made to speak his malapropisms with great clarity and distinctness of utterance. The actor should not be encouraged to imitate Stepin Fetchit.

To think of Mrs. Tiffany as an old battle-axe would not be in error. Though she is sprung from the working-class, her positive enunciation and dynamic energy make probable her acceptance as a leader of fashion. She should be played with relish and demonstrate always her easy assumption of the position of command.

Prudence is a typical old-maid and a busy-body. The actress playing her hasn't much else to go on. Perhaps the best advice is to let her smile a lot and play briskly.

Millinette must be pert and attractive, and her French accent not so thick as to be incomprehensible. This is particularly true of her opening scene with Zeke, when the combination of accents, if poorly enunciated, may simply bewilder the audience.

Gertrude, in virginal white, should contrast markedly with her giddy charge, Seraphina, both in costume and in the manner of playing. Gertrude is everything the personable ward of the sentimental tradition should be: sincere, lovely, unaffected, but mettlesome withal and with a sense of humor. Seraphina, as Millinette says, is a coquette. She should be played by a large girl, and her costume should be over-elaborate as if to compensate for her lack of Gertrude's physical advantages.

FASHION!

or, Life in New York

ACT ONE

The Oleo drop hangs above the first set of wings, "in One." The Drawing Room drop hangs above the third set of wings. R. 3 E. leads to the Conservatory. L. 2 E. leads to the outside hall. Other entrances can be used ad lib. Furniture: A gaudy French chair R.C.; an ornate circular "pouf" or ottoman at L.C. with a removable potted palm with strange flowers on it placed on the post that rises from the centre of the ottoman.

MILLINETTE *is discovered dusting the mantelpiece U.C. with a feather duster. She hums as she works. Crosses to ottoman and dusts that, then the potted palm. She skips across to dust the chair R.C. as* ZEKE *enters L. 2 E.*

ZEKE. (*Cross to* L.C., *regarding his coat.*) Dere's a coat to take de eyes of all Broadway! Tell you what, Missy, (*Cross to* C. *on* R. *of ottoman.*) it am de fixin's dat make de natural-born gemman. A libery forever! (*Indicating his silk knee-pants.*) Dere's a pair of insuppressibles to 'stonish de colored population.

MILLINETTE. (*Cross to below chair, politely.*) Oh, oui, M'sieu Zeke. (*Cross down to footlights* R.C. *Aside.*) I not *comprend* one word he say! (*Skips back to* R. *of chair, giggling.*)

ZEKE. (*Cross 2* R.) I tell 'ee what, Missy, I'm stordinary glad to find dis a bery spectabul like situation! (*Cross to* L. *of chair.*) Now as you've made de acquaint-

8

ance of dis here family, and dere you hab a supernu-
merary advantage of me—seeing dat I receibed mah
appointment dis mo'nin'. What I wants to know is yo'
publicated opinion, privately expressed, of de domestic
circle. (*Backs one step to* L.)

MILLINETTE. (*Cross to his* R. *on* L. *of chair.*) You
mean vat *espèce*, vat kind of *personnes* are M'sieu and
Madame Tiffany? Ah! M'sieu is not ze same t'ing as
Madame—not at all. (*Crossing to* R. *of ottoman, dusts
it.*)

ZEKE. (*Turns* L.) Well, I s'pose he ain't altogether.

MILLINETTE. (*Turns* R. *to him.*) M'sieu is man of business,—Madame is lady of fashion. M'sieu make ze
money,—Madame spend it. M'sieu nobody at all,—
(*Spins in circle.*) Madame everybody altogether.

ZEKE. Yah! Yah! (*Cross* 2 D.R.)

MILLINETTE. (*Cross* R. *to* L. *of* ZEKE.) Ah! M'sieu
Zeke, ze money is all zat is necessaire in zis country to
make one lady of fashion. (*Cross* 2 L.) Oh! It eez quite
anoder t'ing in la belle France!

ZEKE. A bery lucifer explanation. (*Cross* 1 D.R.) Well,
now we've disposed ob de heads ob de family (*Turns
back.*) who come next?

MILLINETTE. (*Cross to* ZEKE'S L.) First, dere is
Mademoiselle Seraphina Tiffany. Mademoiselle eez not
at all one proper *personne.* Mademoiselle Seraphina eez
one coquette. Zat is not zee mode in *la belle France;* zee
ladies dere nevaire learn *la coquetrie* until dey do get
one husband.

ZEKE. (*Crossing her to below* C. *of ottoman.*) I tell 'ee
what, Missy, I done disreprobate dat proceedin' altogether!

MILLINETTE. (*Cross* 2 L.) Vait! I have not tell you all
la famille yet. (ZEKE *stops and turns;* MILLINETTE
cross to his R.) Dere is Ma'mselle Prudence, Madame's
sister, one very *bizarre* personne. Den dere eez Ma'mselle
Gertrude, (*Cross* 1 *down.*) but she nobody at all; she
only teach Mademoiselle Seraphina *la musique,*

ZEKE. (*Cross* 1 *down.*) Well now, Missy, what's yo' own special defunctions?

MILLINETTE. I not understand, M'sieu Zeke.

ZEKE. Den I'll amplifly. (*Cross to her* L. *at* C. *line.*) What's de nature ob yo' exclusive services?

MILLINETTE. *Ah, oui! Je comprend.* (*Cross close to him.*) I am Madame's *femme de chambre.*

ZEKE. Come again?

MILLINETTE. Her lady's maid, M'sieu Zeke.

ZEKE. (*Comprehending.*) Oh!

MILLINETTE. I teach Madame *les modes de Paris,* and Madame set zee fashion for all New York. (*Crossing* R. 2 *and turn back.*) So you see, M'sieu Zeke, dat it is me, *moi-même,* dat do lead zee fashion for all zee American *beau monde!* (*Cross 2* R.)

ZEKE. Yah! Yah! Yah! Ah hab de idea by de heel. Well, now, p'raps you can lustrify mah officials?

MILLINETTE. (*Cross back to him.*) Vat you will have to do? (*Upward inflection.*)

ZEKE. (*Downward inflection.*) Ye-e-e-ah.

MILLINETTE. Oh! much t'ings, much t'ings. (*Ticking them off.*) You vait on ze table,—you tend ze door,—you clean ze boots,—you run ze errands,—you drive ze carriage,—you rub ze horses,—you take care of ze flowers,—you carry ze water,—you help cook ze dinner, —you wash ze dishes,—and den you always remember to do everyt'ing I tell you to! (*Cross away to* R. *of chair.*)

ZEKE. Wheugh, am dat *all?*

MILLINETTE. All I can t'ink of now. (*Cross to him.*) Today is Madame's day of reception, and all her grand friends do make her one *petite* visit. You mind run fast ven ze bell do ring.

ZEKE. Run? If it wasn't for dese superfluminous trimmin's, I tell 'ee what, Missy, I'd run— (*Starts out* L.)

MRS. TIFFANY. (*Off* R.E.) Millinette! (ZEKE *stops;* MILLINETTE *crosses* U.R. *and looks off.*)

MILLINETTE. Here comes Madame! (*Crosses down* C. *to* R. *of* ZEKE.) You better go, M'sieu Zeke.

ZEKE. (*Going* L. 2 E.) Look aheah, Massa Zeke, don't dis open rich! (*Exits* L. 2 E.)

(*Enter* MRS. TIFFANY R. 3 E. *dressed in the most extravagant height of fashion.* MILLINETTE *curtsies from below ottoman as* MRS. TIFFANY *crosses to mantelpiece* U.C. *then down to* L. *of chair.*)

MRS. TIFFANY. Is everything in order, Millinette? Ah! very elegant, very elegant indeed! There is a *jenny-says-quoy* look about this furniture, is there not, Millinette?

MILLINETTE. Oh, *oui*, Madame!

MRS. TIFFANY. (*Crossing down.*) But where is Miss Seraphina? It is twelve o'clock; our visitors will be pouring in! (*Crossing* R. *to* L. *of Chair.*) But I hear that nothing is more fashionable than to keep people waiting. (*Turns.*) Is it not so, Millinette?

MILLINETTE. (*Crosses to* MRS. TIFFANY.) Quite *comme il faut*. Great personnes always do make little personnes wait, Madame.

MRS. TIFFANY. This mode of receiving visitors only upon one specified day of the week is a most convenient custom! (*Crosses* R.) I flatter myself that I was the first to introduce it amongst the New York *ee-light*. (*Turns.*) You are quite sure that it is strictly a Parisian mode, Millinette?

MILLINETTE. (*Crosses* R. *to* C. *line.*) Oh, *oui*, Madame; entirely *mode de Paris*.

MRS. TIFFANY. (*Cross down to footlights, aside.*) This girl is worth her weight in gold. (*Cross up to* U.R. *of chair, indicating it.*) Millinette, how do you say *arm-chair* in French?

MILLINETTE. *Fauteuil*, Madame.

MRS. TIFFANY. *Fow-tool!* That has a foreign sound that is perfectly charming. (*Cross to* U.L. *chair.*) There is something about our American words that is decidedly vulgar. *Fowtool!* How refined. *Arm-chair!* What a difference!

MILLINETTE. (*Cross 1 R.*) Madame have one *charmante* pronunciation. (*Mimicking, aside.*) *Fowtool!* (*Turns R.*) *Charmante*, Madame!

MRS. TIFFANY. (*Adjusting her gloves.*) Do you think so, Millinette? (*Cross 1 L.*) Well, I believe I have. A week's study of that invaluable work—"French Without a Master"—has made me quite at home in the court languages of Europe! (*Crossing down.*) But where is the new valet? (MILLINETTE *crosses L. a step or two indicating Off L.*) What did you say his name was, Millinette? (MILLINETTE *turns back.*)

MILLINETTE. He do say his name is Monsieur Zeke.

MRS. TIFFANY. (*Turns down.*) Zeke! Dear me, such a vulgar name will compromise the dignity of the whole family. (*Turns L.*) Can you not suggest something more aristocratic, Millinette? Something *French!*

MILLINETTE. (*Crossing down to her.*) Oh, *oui*, Madame; *Adolph* is one very fine name.

MRS. TIFFANY. A-dolph! Charming! Ring the bell, Millinette! (MILLINETTE *crosses up to R. of mantelpiece and pulls the painted bell-cord, as* MRS. TIFFANY *crosses R. to R. of ottoman.*) I will change his name immediately, besides giving him a few directions. (*Enter* ZEKE L. 2 E. MRS. TIFFANY *addresses him with great dignity.*) Your name, I hear, is Ezekiel. I consider it too plebeian an appellation to be uttered in my presence. In future you are called A-dolph. (ZEKE *starts to reply;* MRS. TIFFANY *cross L. to him.*) Don't reply,—never interrupt me when I am speaking. (MILLINETTE *smothers a laugh, crosses to* U.R. *chair.*) A-dolph, as my guests arrive, I desire that you inquire the name of every person, and then announce it in a loud, clear tone. *That* is the fashion in Paris. (MRS. TIFFANY *starts R.*)

ZEKE. (*Shouts.*) Consider de office discharged, Missus.

MRS. TIFFANY. (*Cringing, turns L.*) Silence! Your business is to obey and not to speak.

ZEKE. I'm dumb, Missus!

MRS. TIFFANY. (*Looks at chair; smiles, cross to* D.R. *of it, gestures vaguely.*) A-dolph, place that *fow-tool* behind me.

ZEKE. (*Looks around.*) I habn't got dat far in the dictionary yet. No matter, a genus gets his learnin' by nature. (*Takes potted palm from ottoman and starts to place it behind her.*)

MRS. TIFFANY. (*Backing* R. *a step.*) You dolt! Where have you lived not to know that *fow-tool* is the French for *arm-chair?* What ignorance! Leave the room this instant!

(ZEKE *puts palm back.* MILLINETTE *pushes chair forward and* MRS. TIFFANY *sits as* ZEKE *exits.*)

ZEKE. (*As he exits.*) Dem's de defects ob not having a libery education. (*Exits* L. 2 E.)

MRS. TIFFANY. Thank you, Millinette.

(PRUDENCE *peeps in,* L. 3 E.)

PRUDENCE. I wonder if any of the fine folks have come yet. (*Crosses down.*) Not a soul. I knew they hadn't. There's Lizzy all alone. (*Cross to* C.) Sister Lizzy!

MRS. TIFFANY. (*Seated.*) Prudence! How many times have I desired you to call me *Elizabeth? Lizzy* is the height of vulgarity.

PRUDENCE. Oh, I forgot. (*Crossing* U.C. *and turning down.*) Dear me, how spruce we do look here, to be sure —everything in first-rate style now, Lizzy. (PRUDENCE *cross to* L. *of chair.* MRS. TIFFANY *looks at her angrily.* MILLINETTE *crosses up and pretends to dust* L. *side mantelpiece.*) Elizabeth I mean. Who would have thought, when you and I were sitting behind that little counter in Canal Street, making up flashy hats and caps . . .

MRS. TIFFANY. (*Rises.*) Prudence, what *do* you mean?

(*Cross* L. *to* R. *of* MILLINETTE.) Millinette, leave the room.

MILLINETTE. *Oui,* Madame. (*She crosses to* L. *of ottoman and peeps out between the leaves as* MRS. TIFFANY *crosses down a step toward* PRUDENCE.)

PRUDENCE. I always said you were destined to rise above your station, Lizzy.

MRS. TIFFANY. (*Cross to* L. *of* PRUDENCE.) Prudence! Have I not told you that . . .

PRUDENCE. No, Lizzy, it was *I* that told *you,* when we used to buy our silks and ribbons of Mr. Antony Tiffany, (*Makes a jawing movement with her fingers.*) "*talking Tony,*" you know we used to call him, and when you always put on the finest bonnet in our shop to go to his . . . (MILLINETTE *cross to below* C. *of ottoman.*) I always told you that *something* would grow out of it— and didn't it?

MRS. TIFFANY. (*Cross to* L. *as* PRUDENCE *cross to up of chair.*) Millinette, send Seraphina here instantly. Leave the room.

MILLINETTE. (*Crossing to* D.R.C. *close to foots for aside.*) Oui, Madame. (*Aside.*) So dis Americaine lady of fashion vas one *milliner?* Oh, vat a fine country for *les merchandes des modes!* I shall send for all my relations by zee next packet! (*Exits* R. 2 E.)

MRS. TIFFANY. (*Crossing to* L. *of* PRUDENCE.) Prudence! Never let me hear you mention this subject again. Forget what we *have* been, it is enough to remember that we *are* of the upper *ten thousand!* (*Cross* 1 L.)

(*Enter* SERAPHINA R. 2 E. *Tiptoes affectedly on, crossing to* L. *of* MRS. TIFFANY *who holds* R. *of* C. *line.* SERAPHINA *turns, showing her dress.*)

MRS. TIFFANY. Ah! Seraphina! How bewitchingly you look, my dear! (*Approaching her, and with some misgivings.*) Does Millinette say that that head dress is strictly Parisian?

SERAPHINA. (*Loudly.*) Oh yes, Mamma, all the rage!

MRS. TIFFANY. (*Drawing* SERAPHINA *down to front* L.C.) Now, Seraphina my dear, don't be too particular in your attentions to gentlemen not eligible. There is Count *Jolly-may-tra,* decidedly the most fashionable foreigner in town, and so refined. You may devote yourself to him.

SERAPHINA. Yes, Mamma. (*Crosses to* C. *of ottoman and sits.*)

ZEKE. (*Entering* L. 2 E., *loudly.*) Mister T. Tennyson Twinkle!

MRS. TIFFANY. (*Grimacing.*) Show him up. (ZEKE *exits* L. 2 E.)

PRUDENCE. I must be running away! (*Exits* R. 2 E.)

MRS. TIFFANY. (*Advancing to front, speaks directly to audience.*) Mr. T. Tennyson Twinkle—a very literary young man and a sweet poet! It's all the rage to patronize poets! (*Points to magazine on ottoman. Crosses* R. *to chair and sits.*) Quick, Seraphina, hand me that magazine. Mr. Twinkle writes for it. (SERAPHINA *crosses and hands it to her, then resumes her seat on the ottoman.* MRS. TIFFANY *pretends to read.*)

ZEKE. (*At* L. 2 E.) Mr. T. Tennyson Twinkle!

TWINKLE. (*Enters* L. 2 E. ZEKE *exits.* TWINKLE *cross to* L. *of* SERAPHINA, *takes her hand, kneels.*)

Fair Seraphina! the sun itself grows dim,
Unless you aid his light and shine on him!

SERAPHINA. (*As* TWINKLE *rises and kisses her hand.*) Ah! Mr. Twinkle, there is no such thing as answering you.

TWINKLE. (*Perceiving* MRS. TIFFANY, *crosses to her and reads over her shoulder.*) Aha! Mrs. Tiffany! (*Aside.*) "The New Monthly Vernal Galaxy." Reading my verses by all that's charming! Sensible woman! I won't interrupt her. (*Starts cross to* L.)

MRS. TIFFANY. Ah! Mr. Twinkle, is that you? I was perfectly *abimé* at the perusal of your very *distingué* verses.

TWINKLE. I am overwhelmed, Madame. Permit me (*Taking the magazine.*) Yes, they do read tolerably. And

you must take into consideration, ladies, the rapidity
with which they were written. Four minutes and a half
by the stop-watch! The true test of a poet is the velocity
with which he composes. Really they do look very
prettily, and they read *very* tolerably—especially the
first verse. (*Reads.*) "To Seraphina T. . . ." (*Cross 2
L.*)

SERAPHINA. Oh! Mr. Twinkle!

TWINKLE. (*Sets himself and recites.*) "Around my
heart"—

MRS. TIFFANY. (*Loudly.*) How touching! Really, Mr.
Twinkle, quite tender!

TWINKLE. (*Recommencing.*) "Around my heart"—

MRS. TIFFANY. Oh, I must tell you, Mr. Twinkle! I
heard the other day that poets were the aristocrats of
literature. That's one reason I like 'em, for I do dote on
all aristocracy!

TWINKLE. Oh, Madame, how flattering! (*Cross to* C.)
Now pray lend me your ears! (*Reads.*)
        "Around my heart thou weavest"—

SERAPHINA. That is such a *sweet* commencement, Mr.
Twinkle!

TWINKLE. (*Cross 1 step down, aside.*) I wish she
wouldn't interrupt me! (*Returns to position. Reads.*)
        "Around my heart thou weavest a spell"—

MRS. TIFFANY. (*Rising.*) Beautiful! But excuse me
one moment while I say a word to Seraphina. (*She
crosses to* R. *of* SERAPHINA *as* TWINKLE *drops to* D.R.)
Don't be too affable, my dear! Poets are very ornamental
appendages to the drawing room, but they're always as
poor as their own verses. They don't make eligible
husbands! (*Turns and crosses back to chair.*) Now, Mr.
Twinkle!

TWINKLE. (*On* R. *of chair.*) My dear Madam, unless
you pay the utmost attention you cannot catch the ideas.
Are you ready?

MRS. TIFFANY. (*Sitting in the chair.*) Quite!

TWINKLE. (*Crossing to* C.) Well, now you shall hear
it to the end! (*Reads.*)

"Around my heart thou weavest a spell,
Whose"--

ZEKE. (*Entering* L. 2 E.) Mister Augustus Fogg! (*Aside.*) A bery misty-lookin' gemman!

MRS. TIFFANY. Show him up, Adolph! (ZEKE *exits.*)

TWINKLE. (*Crossing to* U.C.) This is too much!

SERAPHINA. Exquisite verses, Mr. Twinkle,--exquisite!

TWINKLE. (*Coming down to her* R.) Ah, lovely Seraphina! Your smile of approval transports me to the summit of Olympus. (*He sits down next to her.*)

SERAPHINA. Then I must frown, for I would not send you so far away.

TWINKLE. (*He leans in close to her.*) Enchantress! (*Rises, aside.*) It's all over with her. (*Crosses* U.C. *to mantelpiece.*)

ZEKE. (*Enters* L. 2 E. *announcing.*) Mr. Augustus Fogg! (FOGG *enters* L. 2 E. *and holds* D.L.C. *striking a pose, as* ZEKE *exits* L. 2 E.)

MRS. TIFFANY. (*Rises, comes down, speaks rapidly and without a breath to audience as she points to* FOGG.) Mr. Fogg belongs to one of our oldest families,--to be sure he is the most difficult person in the world to entertain for he never takes the trouble to talk and never notices anything or anybody but then I hear that nothing is considered so vulgar as to betray any emotion or to attempt to render oneself agreeable. (*Turns* L.) Ah! Mr. Fogg!

FOGG. (*Crosses* R. *to* L. *of* MRS. TIFFANY, *bows stiffly.*) Mrs. Tiffany, your most obedient. (*Turns* L. *to address* SERAPHINA *but stays* R. *of* TWINKLE.) Miss Seraphina, yours. (*Extends two fingers as hand-shake to* TWINKLE.) How d'ye do, Twinkle.

MRS. TIFFANY. Fine weather, Mr. Fogg,--delightful, isn't it?

FOGG. (*Facing front.*) I am indifferent to weather, Madam.

MRS. TIFFANY. Been to the opera, Mr. Fogg? (*Cross to chair.*) I hear the *bow monde* make their *debutt* there every evening. (*Sits chair.*)

Fogg. I consider operas a bore, Madam.

Seraphina. You must hear Mr. Twinkle's verses, Mr. Fogg!

Fogg. (*Crossing* L. *below ottoman to* L. *of it.*) I am indifferent to verses, Miss Seraphina.

Seraphina. But Mr. Twinkle's verses are addressed to me!

Twinkle. (*At* R. *of ottoman.*) Now pay attention, Fogg! (Fogg *sits* L. *side ottoman.*)
> "Around my heart, thou weavest a spell
> Whose magic I . . ."

(*Enter* Zeke L. 2 E.)

Zeke. (*Announcing.*) Mister— No, he say he ain't no Mister—

Twinkle.
> "Around my heart, thou weavest a spell
> Whose magic I can never tell. . . ."

Mrs. Tiffany. (*Rising.*) Speak in a loud, clear tone, A-dolph!

Twinkle. (*Crossing up to drop.*) This is terrible!

Zeke. Mister Count Jolly-made-her!

Mrs. Tiffany. Count Jolly-may-tra! Good gracious! (*Cross* L. *to* C.) Zeke, Zeke—A-dolph I mean— (*Aside.*) Dear me what a mistake! Set that chair out of the way! (Zeke *crosses* R. *and pretends to move chair.*) Seraphina, my dear, (*Pulls* Seraphina *off the ottoman and places her on her* R. Zeke *below* R. *of chair moves in close to* Seraphina.) are you all in order? Dear me! dear me! Your dress is so tumbled! (*Dress bus. To* Zeke.) What are you grinning at? Beg the Count to honor us by walking up. (Zeke *exits* L. 3 E. *going above ottoman.* Mrs. Tiffany *pulls* Seraphina *further Downstage and to* R. *as* Fogg *rises and stands in entrance* L. 2 E.) Seraphina, my dear, remember now what I told you about the Count. He is a man of the highest . . . good gracious! I am so flurried; and nothing is so ungenteel as agitation! what will the Count think! (*Crosses up to* Twinkle *and pushes him far down* R.) Mr. Twinkle, pray stand out of the way. (*Cross to* L. *of* SERAPHINA.) Seraphina, my dear, place yourself on my right! (*Crossing* L. *to* FOGG.) Mr. Fogg, the conservatory! (*Pulling him* R.; *he resists.*) Beautiful flowers—pray amuse yourself in the conservatory. (*Indicates* U.R.)

FOGG. I am indifferent to flowers, Madam.

MRS. TIFFANY. (*Crosses to* D.C. *Aside.*) Dear me! the man stands right in the way,—just where the Count must make his *entray!* Mr. Fogg! Pray . . . !

(*Enter* ZEKE L. 2 E., *stands just above* FOGG *blocking the way.*)

ZEKE. Count Jolly-made-her!

(*Enter* COUNT JOLIMAITRE L. 2 E. *Bus.* COUNT *trying to get by* ZEKE *and* FOGG. TWINKLE *drops down* R.C. *on* R. *of* SERAPHINA.)

MRS. TIFFANY. Oh, Count, this unexpected honor! . . .

SERAPHINA. Count, this inexpressible pleasure! . . .

COUNT. (*Finally extricates himself and crosses* R. *to* L. *of* MRS. TIFFANY *as* ZEKE *exits.*) Beg you won't mention it, Madam! (*Crosses* R. *to* SERAPHINA *as* MRS. TIFFANY *slides along above him to keep herself between them.*) Miss Seraphina, your most devoted!

MRS. TIFFANY. (*Her head between theirs, aside.*) What condescension! (COUNT *and* SERAPHINA *step back, enlarging the triangle.*) Count, may I take the liberty to introduce . . . (*Indicates* TWINKLE *who advances to* R. *of* MRS. TIFFANY. *The men are about to shake hands when* MRS. TIFFANY *inserts herself between them. Aside.*) Good gracious! I forgot. Count, I was about to remark that we never introduce in America. (TWINKLE *turns away in high dudgeon to* D.R.)

COUNT. Excuse me, Madam, our fashions have grown antediluvian before you Americans discover their existence. (*Looking at* FOGG *through monocle.*) You are lamentably behind the age—lamentably! 'Pon my honor, a foreigner of refinement finds great difficulty in existing in this provincial atmosphere.

MRS. TIFFANY. How dreadful, Count! If there is anything I can do . . .

SERAPHINA. (*Below chair.*) Or I, Count, to render your situation less deplorable . . .

COUNT. (*Crosses* R. *to* SERAPHINA.) Ah! I find but one redeeming charm in America . . . (*Looking her up and down.*) . . . the superlative loveliness of the feminine portion of creation . . . (*Aside, stepping down.*) and the wealth of their obliging papa.

MRS. TIFFANY. (*At* COUNT'S L.) How flattering! Ah! Count, I am afraid you will turn the head of my simple girl here. She is a perfect child of nature, Count.

COUNT. (*Looking somewhat lasciviously at* SERAPHINA.) Very possibly. (*To* MRS. TIFFANY.) For though you American women are quite charming, yet, demme, there's a deal of native rust to rub off. (COUNT *cross* R. *to chair.*)

MRS. TIFFANY. *Rust!* (*Crossing* U.C. *on* R. *of ottoman, looking around the room.*) Good gracious, Count! Where do you find any rust?

COUNT. (*To front, as he sits in chair.*) How very unsophisticated!

MRS. TIFFANY. (*Returning to* COUNT'S L.) Count, I am so ashamed, pray excuse me! Although a lady of large fortune, and one who can boast of the highest connections, I blush to confess that I have never travelled. While you, Count, I presume are at home in all the courts of Europe.

COUNT. (*Rising in alarm.*) *Courts!* Eh? (*Recovering himself.*) Oh, yes, Madam, very true. I believe I *am* pretty well known in some of the courts of Europe—(*Crossing down to front, aside.*) *police courts.* (*Crossing up to* L. *of* MRS. TIFFANY.) In a word, Madam, I had seen enough of civilized life—wanted to refresh myself by a sight of barbarous countries and customs—had my

choice between the Sandwich Islands and New York—
chose New York!

MRS. TIFFANY. (*To* SERAPHINA.) How complimentary
to our country! And, Count, I have no doubt you speak
every conceivable language? You talk English like a
native!

COUNT. (*Lapsing into Cockney.*) Eh, wot? Loike a
nytive? (*Recovering his Oxford accent.*) Oh, ah, demme,
yes, I *am* something of an Englishman. Passed one year
and eight months with the Duke of Wellington; six
months with Lord Brougham; two and a half with Count
d'Orsay—knew them all more intimately than their best
friends— (*Close to her* L.) no heroes to me—hadn't a
secret from me, I assure you,— (*Aside.*) especially of the
toilet. (*Sits on* R. *side of ottoman.*)

MRS. TIFFANY. (*Joining* SERAPHINA *by chair.*) Think
of that, my dear! Lord Wellington and Dook Broom.

SERAPHINA. (*Aside.*) And only think of Count d'Orsay,
Mamma! (*Crosses to* R. *of* COUNT *who remains seated.*)
I am so wild to see Count d'Orsay!

COUNT. A mere man milliner. Very little refinement
out of Paris. Why, at the very last dinner given by Lord
—Lord Knowswho, would you believe it, Madame, there
was an individual present who wore a *black* cravat and
took *soup twice!*

MRS. TIFFANY. (*Crossing to* R. *of* SERAPHINA.) How
shocking! The sight of him would have spoilt me ap-
petite! (*Draws* SERAPHINA *a step to* R. *Aside.*) Think
what a great man he must be, my dear, to despise lords
and counts in that way. (*To front.*) I must leave them
together. (*Crossing* R. *to* TWINKLE, *gives him her arm
and spins him counter-clockwise so that he ends* U.R.
near R. 3 E.) Mr. Twinkle, your arm. I have some really
very *foreign exotics* to show you.

TWINKLE. I fly at your command. (MRS. TIFFANY
freezes at C. *Aside.*) I wish all her exotics were blooming
in their native soil!

MRS. TIFFANY. (*Crosses to* FOGG *as* COUNT *takes*
SERAPHINA *Upstage above ottoman.*) Mr. Fogg, will you

accompany us? My conservatory—well worth a visit—it cost an immense amount . . . (*Pulling him.*)

FOGG. I am indifferent to conservatories, Madam; flowers are such a bore!

MRS. TIFFANY. (*Pulling him off* U.R.; R. 3 E.) I shall take no refusal. Conservatories are all the rage—I could not exist without mine! Let me show you. (*They exit;* MRS. TIFFANY *returns and drags* TWINKLE *off, saying . . .*) Let me show you!

SERAPHINA. (*Cross down and sits on ottoman.*) America, then, has no charms for you, Count?

COUNT. (*On her Right, puts foot up on ottoman and bends over her.*) Excuse me—some exceptions. I find you, for instance, particularly charming! Can't say I admire your country. (*Foot down.*) Ah! If you had ever breathed the exhilarating air of Paris, ate creams at Tortoni's, dined at the Café Royale . . . or if you had lived in London—felt at home at St. James's, and every afternoon driven a couple of Lords and a Duchess through Hyde Park, you would find America—where you have no kings, queens, lords, nor ladies—insupportable!

SERAPHINA. (*Flirtatiously.*) Not while there was a Count in it!

(*Enter* ZEKE, *very indignant, crosses to* C.)

ZEKE. Where's de Missus?

(*Enter* MRS. TIFFANY, TWINKLE *and* FOGG *from* R. 3 E.)

MRS. TIFFANY. (*On* ZEKE'S R.) Whom do you come to announce, A-dolph?

ZEKE. He said he wouldn't trust me—not eben wid his name; so I wouldn't trust him upstairs; den he ups wid *his stick* and ah *cuts mine!*

MRS. TIFFANY. (*Down a step for aside.*) Some of Mr. Tiffany's vulgar acquaintances! I shall die with shame. A-dolph, inform him that I am *not at home!* (ZEKE *exits* L. 2 E. *crossing above ottoman.*) My nerves are so shattered, I'm ready to sink. (*Totters to below chair on* R.C.) Mr. Twinkle, that *fow-tool,* if you please!

TWINKLE. (*Over her* L. *shoulder.*) What? What do you wish, Madam?

MRS. TIFFANY. (*Aside.*) The ignorance of these Americans! (*Crossing* L. *to* R. *of* COUNT.) Count, may I trouble you? That *fow-tool,* if you please!

COUNT. (*A step down, aside.*) She's not talking English, nor French, but I suppose it's American.

TRUEMAN. (*Off* L.) Not at home!

ZEKE. (*Off.*) No, sar—Missus say she's not at home.

TRUEMAN. (*Off.*) Out of my way, you grinning baboon!

(*Enter* ADAM TRUEMAN L. 3 E., *a stout cane in his hand. Crosses to* D.L., *looking around him.*)

TRUEMAN. Where's this woman that's not *at home* in her own house? May I be shot! if I wonder at it! I shouldn't think she'd *ever* feel *at home* in such a show-box as this!

MRS. TIFFANY. (*Crossing down, aside.*) What a plebeian looking old farmer! I wonder who he is? (*Cross* 1 L.) Sir! What do you mean, Sir, by this *ow*dacious conduct? (*Shuffling in agitation.*) How dare you intrude yourself into my parlor? Do you know who I am, Sir? (*With great dignity.*) You are in the presence of Mrs. Tiffany, Sir!

TRUEMAN. (*Crosses* R. *to* L. *of* MRS. TIFFANY, *crossing* COUNT.) Antony's wife, eh? Well now I might have guessed it—ha! ha! ha!—for I see you make it a point to carry half your husband's shop upon your back! (COUNT *crosses around ottoman and emerges* L. *of it.*)

MRS. TIFFANY. (*Furious.*) How dare you! (*Aside.*) What will the Count think!

TRUEMAN. Why, I thought folks had better manners in the city! This is a civil welcome for your husband's old friend; and after my coming all the way from Catteraugus just to see you and yours!

Mrs. Tiffany. Catteraugus! Ugh! (*Aside.*) How shall I get rid of him?

Trueman. (*Crossing to* R. *of* Seraphina *who remains seated on ottoman. Aside.*) I hope that this is not Gertrude!

Mrs. Tiffany. (*Crossing up to* R. *of* Trueman.) Sir, I'd have you know that . . . Seraphina, my child, walk with the gentlemen into the conservatory. (*Exeunt* Seraphina, Twinkle *and* Fogg R. 3 E. Mrs. Tiffany *crosses* L. *to* R. *of* Count *leaving* Trueman U.C.) Count Jolly-may-tra, pray make due allowance for the errors of this rustic! I do assure you, Count . . . (*Whispers to him.*)

Trueman. (*To front.*) Count! She calls that critter with a shoe brush over his mouth, Count! To look at him, I should have thought he was a tailor's walking advertisement! (*Crosses down to* R.C.)

Count. (*Who has been inspecting* Trueman *through his eye-glass, crosses to* L. *of* Trueman.) Where did you say you belonged, my friend? Dug out of the ruins of Pompeii, eh? (Mrs. Tiffany *remains below ottoman, close to it.*)

Trueman. I belong to a land in which I rejoice to find that you are a foreigner.

Count. What a barbarian! He doesn't see the honor I'm doing his country! (*Crosses to* Mrs. Tiffany.) Pray, Madam, is it one of the aboriginal inhabitants of the soil? To what tribe of Indians does he belong—the Pawnee or the Choctaw? (*Approaches* Trueman *again.*) Do you carry a tomahawk?

Trueman. Something quite as useful,—do you see that? (*Shakes his stick, chases* Count *around* L. *of ottoman, going above it, and across the Stage so that* Count *stops* U.R. *of chair and* Trueman *at centre.*)

Mrs. Tiffany. (*During uproar staggers to ottoman and sits.*) Oh, dear! I shall faint! Millinette! Millinette!

Millinette. (*Entering* R. 2 E., *crosses below* Count *to* R.C.) Oui, Madame?

Mrs. Tiffany. A glass of water! (Millinette *exits*

R. 2 E.) Sir! (*Rises.*) Sir, I am shocked at your plebeian conduct! This is a gentleman of the highest standing, Sir! He is a *Count*, Sir!

(MILLINETTE *enters* R. 2 E. *bearing a glass of water on a salver. She crosses the* COUNT, *stops at* R.C., *does a double take.* COUNT *looks at her and crosses* D.R. *hiding his face with a handkerchief.* MILLINETTE *points to* COUNT *and screams.* COUNT *regains his composure, dusts himself with handkerchief, looks unconcerned.*)

MRS. TIFFANY. What is the matter? What *is* the matter!

MILLINETTE. Not'ing, not'ing—only— (*Drinks water.*) not'ing at all!

TRUEMAN. (*On her* L.) Don't be afraid, girl. Did you never see a live Count before? He's tame,—I daresay your mistress here leads him about by the ears.

MRS. TIFFANY. (*Sinking down on* R. *of ottoman.*) This is too much! Millinette, send for Mr. Tiffany instantly!

MILLINETTE. (*Crosses to* L. 3 E., *sees* MR. TIFFANY *off.*) He just come in, Madame! (*Exits* L. 3 E.)

TRUEMAN. My old friend! Where is he? Take me to him! (MR. TIFFANY *enters* L. 3 E. *in hang-dog manner, crosses slowly to* D.L.C. *as* TRUEMAN *crosses to him.*) Ah! Here he is! How I've longed to have one more shake of your hand! (*Takes* MR. TIFFANY's *limp hand and pumps it vigorously.*) Little Antony, my excellent friend! But what a change is here!

MRS. TIFFANY. (*Crossing to* COUNT.) Count, honor me by joining my daughter in the conservatory, I will return immediately. (*Swings the* COUNT *up and off* R. 3 E.) Antony! (MR. TIFFANY *timidly crosses to her at* C. *where they whisper.*)

TRUEMAN. (D.L.C.) What a Jezebel! These women always play the very devil with a man, and yet I don't believe such a damaged bale of goods as *that* (*Indicat-*

ing MRS. TIFFANY.) has smothered the heart of little Antony!

MRS. TIFFANY. (*Indicating by her change in manner that* MR. TIFFANY *has told her of* MR. TRUEMAN'S *wealth and former helpfulness, crosses* L. *to* C., *indicates* R. 3 E.) This way, Sir! (*Curtseys.*) Sal vooz plate! Come, Antony! (*Beckons* MR. TIFFANY *who exits before her, she following out* R. 3 E.)

TRUEMAN. (*Crossing to* C.) Sal vooz plate!? Ha, ha, ha! We shall see what Fashion has done for him. (*Starts exit cross to* R. 3 E. *as CURTAIN falls.*)

MUSICAL SELECTION: "Walking Down Broadway," THE COUNT.

(*The number is staged before the Oleo Curtain during the scene change. It is an appropriate number for the* COUNT, *although in the Yale production it was sung by a trio composed of the* COUNT, MRS. TIFFANY, *and* SERAPHINA, *as indicated below.*)

COUNT. (*Enter* L. 1 E., *singing. Carries cane, wears white gloves and a top hat. Crosses to* L.C.)

    1. Walking down Broadway,
       The festive, gay Broadway.
       The O.K. thing on Saturday,
       Is walking down Broadway. (*Crosses to* C.)
    2. Walking down Broadway,
       The festive, gay Broadway.
       The O.K. thing on Saturday,
       Is walking down Broadway. (*Walking to* L.C.)

MRS. TIFFANY—SERAPHINA. (*Enter* R. *singing. Cross to* R.C. COUNT *gesticulates as if introducing them to audience.*)

    3. Walking down Broadway

        (*Repeat Chorus*)

(COUNT — MRS. TIFFANY — SERAPHINA *then repeat Chorus for the fourth time. As they do so,* COUNT *crosses to* R., MRS. TIFFANY *and* SERAPHINA *to* L., *bowing to each other as if meeting on the street. They then cross back to* C. *and* COUNT *places himself between them. From this* C. *position they sing the first verse:*

> The sweetest thing in life
> And no one dare say nay,
> On a Saturday afternoon
> Is Walking Down Broadway.
> Our good friends in the Park
> Or at Long Branch wish to stray
> But we prefer to walk
> Down the festive gay Broadway.

(*Music out.* COUNT *advances a step, removing his hat. Speaks.*)

COUNT. And I must say, ladies and gentlemen, with all due deference to the other pleasures in life, there is nothing quite so charming as . . . (*All singing and walking* L. *in unison.*)

> 5. Walking Down Broadway, etc.
> 6. Walking Down Broadway, etc.

(*All walk to* R. 1 E. *On last line all exit* R.)

* * *

Encore

SERAPHINA. (*Enters, crosses to* R.C.)
> Walking down Broadway,

COUNT. (*Joins her, singing.*)
> The festive gay Broadway,

MRS. TIFFANY. (*Enters singing to* R. *of* COUNT.)
The O.K. thing on Saturday
Is walking down Broadway.

(*They repeat the Chorus for the last time as they cross*
L. *to* C., *circle cross up and return to* R., *whispering
last line as they exit* R.)

ACT TWO

Scene 1

Inner apartment of Mr. Tiffany's *Counting House. The backdrop shows a gloomy room with cracked walls. Ledgers and files are painted on the drop. The* c. *entrance is an opening cut in the drop. A low desk, covered with papers and bills, is placed* R. *of the* c. *door with a chair behind it on which* Mr. Tiffany *sits. To the* L. *of the door and in profile is a high desk with a stool on the* R. *of it. On the stool sits* Mr. Snobson *entering figures in a large ledger. His coat and hat are hung on a hook on the* L. *side of his desk. As the CURTAIN rises,* Mr. Tiffany *groans at the weight of bills confronting him, and* Mr. Snobson *laughs sardonically at his employer's plight.*

Snobson. How the old boy frets and fumes over those papers! (Mr. Tiffany *groans.*) To be sure! (*Another groan from* Mr. Tiffany.) He's working himself up into a perfect fever! (Mr. Tiffany *rises, clutching his head.*) Exactly! (Mr. Tiffany *exits* R.) Therefore bleeding's the prescription! (Snobson *rises and crosses down to the front of the stage, addressing audience.*) I have him in my clutches. He's tried many times to squirm out of my grasp. But he ain't smart enough for Joe; no, not for Joe Snobson! (*MUSIC: "Not for Joe."*)

> Joseph Snobson is my name,
> My friends all call me Joe.
> I'm up you know to every game,
> And everything I know.
> I once was green as green could be,
> I suffered for it though.
> Now if they try it on with me,
> I tell 'em "Not for Joe!"

Chorus:

> Not for Joe, not for Joe,
> If he knows it, not for Joseph.
> No, no, no, not for Joe,
> Not for Joseph, Oh dear, no!

> There's a fellow called Jack Bannister;
> He's the sort of chap, is Jack,
> Who's always borrowing money,
> But he never pays it back. (*Vindictively.*)
> Last Thursday night he comes to me,
> Says he's just got back to town,
> And bein' rather short of cash, (*Imitating Jack.*)
> Could I lend him half a crown?

(*Spoken.*) "Well," says I—more in sorrow than in anger
—"if I thought I might get it back again, I would with
pleasure. But you'll excuse me if I say . . .

Chorus:

> Not for Joe, etc.

> I think he's had enough of Joe,
> Decline I really must,
> He'd thank me for my kindness though,
> If I would only trust.
> Ah, "trust," my boy! It's trust too long
> Your favor to retain;—
> Perhaps now, as you know my song,
> I needn't sing again. . . .

Chorus:

> Not for Joe, etc.

(*Slower tempo;* SNOBSON *looking guiltily into the wings*
L. and R.)

> There's a friend of mine at (*York and Wall*),
>   (*Substitute local street names.*)
> The other night says: "Joe,
> I'll introjuice you to a gal,
> You really ought to know.
> She's a widow you should try and win,—
> 'Twould a good match be for you—

She's pretty and got lots o' tin, (*Sweetly.*)
And only fifty-two."
(*Spoken, in loud disdain.*) Think of that! Fifty-two! Old enough to be my grandmother. (*Confidentially.*) And you know a fellow can't marry his grandmother. . . . Lots of tin, though, and pretty . . . (*Shouting.*) Fifty-two! No. . . .

    Chorus:

    Not for Joe, etc.

(*On last line of song he strides back to stool and sits.
    MR. TIFFANY re-enters R. and sits at his desk.
    SNOBSON rises and crosses to R.C.*)

SNOBSON. Mr. Tiffany, a word with you, if you please, Sir!

TIFFANY. (*At desk.*) Speak on, Mr. Snobson, I attend.

SNOBSON. What I have to say, Sir, is a matter of first importance to the credit of the concern— (*Swings his head close to MR. TIFFANY'S.*) the *credit* of the concern, Mr. Tiffany!

TIFFANY. Proceed, Mr. Snobson.

SNOBSON. Sir, you've a handsome house—fine carriage —servants in livery—feed on the fat of the land—everything first-rate. . . .

TIFFANY. Well, Sir?

SNOBSON. (*Threateningly.*) My salary, Mr. Tiffany!

TIFFANY. (*Rising to L. of chair.*) It has been raised three times within the last year.

SNOBSON. Still, it is insufficient for the necessities of an honest man, (*Stepping back.*) mark me, an *honest* man, Mr. Tiffany.

TIFFANY. (*Comes forward for aside to audience,* L.C.) What a weapon he has made of that word! (*Crosses back to* L. *of* SNOBSON.) Enough—another hundred shall be added. Does that content you?

SNOBSON. (*Rubbing his hands.*) There is another subject which I have before mentioned, Mr. Tiffany, (*With leering emphasis.*) —your daughter! What's the reason you can't let the folks at home know at once that I'm to be *the man?*

TIFFANY. (*Down a step, to audience.*) Villain! And must the only seal upon this scoundrel's lips be placed there by the hand of my daughter? (*Back to* SNOBSON.) Well, Sir, it shall be as you desire.

SNOBSON. (*Following up his advantage.*) And Mrs. Tiffany shall be informed of your resolution?

TIFFANY. (*Brokenly.*) Yes. (*Crosses* R. *to* D.R.C.)

SNOBSON. (*Triumphantly.*) Enough said! That's the ticket! The *credit* of the *concern* is now safe, Sir! (*Hums "Not For Joe" as he returns to his stool.*)

TIFFANY. (*Below desk to audience.*) How low have I bowed to this insolent rascal! To rise himself he mounts upon my shoulders, and unless I can shake him off he must crush me!

(*Enter* TRUEMAN *at* C. *door.*)

TRUEMAN. Here I am, Antony, man! (TIFFANY *does a startled double-take.*) I told you I'd pay a visit to your money-making quarters. (*Crossing down a step to* L.C.) But it looks as dismal here as a cell in the States' Prison!

TIFFANY. (*Shudders, forces a laugh, crosses up to* R. *of chair at desk.*) Ha, ha, ha! States' Prison! You are so facetious! Ha, ha! (*Mirthlessly.*)

TRUEMAN. Well, I can't see anything so amusing in that! I should think the States' Prison plaguy uncomfortable lodgings. (*Crosses* R. *to* L. *of chair at desk.*) And you laugh, man, as though you fancied yourself there already.

TIFFANY. (*Painfully.*) Ha, ha, ha! (*Sits at desk.*)

TRUEMAN. (*Imitating him.*) Ha, ha, ha! What do you mean by that ill-sounding laugh that has nothing of a laugh about it! This *fashion*-worship has made hypocrites of you all! I have lived in your house only three days, and I have heard more lies than were ever invented during a Presidential election! First, your fine lady of a wife sends me word that she's not at home—I walk upstairs,

and she takes good care that I shall not feel *at home.*
Then *you* come in—take your old friend by the hand—
whisper the deuce knows what in your wife's ear, and
the tables are turned in a tangent! Madam curtsies—
says she's enchanted to see me—and extends all the
hospitality of the house.

TIFFANY. (*Rising, crosses to below* R.C. *of desk.*) We
were exceedingly happy to welcome you as our guest.

TRUEMAN. (*Crosses to* TIFFANY.) Happy? *You,*
happy? (*Puts his arm on* TIFFANY'S *shoulder.*) Ah!
Antony! Antony! that hatchet face of yours, and those
criss-cross furrows tell quite another story! (*Backs to*
U.L. *edge desk.*) Your warm heart has grown cold over
your ledgers—your light spirits heavy with calculations!
You have traded away your youth—your hopes—your
tastes—for wealth! And now that you *have* the wealth
you coveted, what does it profit you? Pleasure it cannot
buy; ease it will not bring. It has made your counting-
house a *penitentiary* and your home a fashionable
museum where there is no niche for you! See me, man!
seventy-two last August!—strong as hickory and every
whit as sound! (*Backs to* U.C.)

TIFFANY. (*Crossing to* L. *edge desk.*) I take the
greatest pleasure in remarking your superiority, Sir.

TRUEMAN. Bah! No man takes pleasure in remarking
the superiority of another! Why the deuce can't you
speak the truth, man? But it's not the *fashion,* I suppose.
(*Crossing* D.R. *to* R. *of* TIFFANY.) I have not seen one
frank, open face since—no, no, I can't say that either,
though lying is catching . . . (*MUSIC Cue,—a snatch
of "Hearts and Flowers."*) There is that girl, Gertrude,
who is trying to teach your daughter music—but
Gertrude was bred in the country! (*MUSIC out.*)

TIFFANY. (*Returns to chair and sits.*) A good girl; my
wife and I find her very useful.

TRUEMAN. *Useful!* Well I must say you have queer
notions of *use!* (*Crosses up to* R. *of* TIFFANY *at desk.*)
But come, cheer up, man! I'd rather see one of your old
smiles than know you'd realized another thousand!

(*Crosses above desk chair to* L. *of* TIFFANY, *pushing the backdrop aside to get by, if he has to.*) I hear you're making money in the true, American, high-pressure style—better go slow and sure—the more steam, the greater danger of the boiler's bursting! All sound, I hope? Nothing rotten at the core?

TIFFANY. (*With a sickly expression.*) Oh, sound— quite sound!

TRUEMAN. Well, that's pleasant—though I must say you don't look very pleasant about it!

TIFFANY. (*Rising.*) My good friend, although I am solvent, I may say perfectly solvent—yet you . . . the fact is, you *can* be of some assistance to me!

TRUEMAN. That's the *fact,* is it? I'm glad we've hit upon one *fact* at last! Well . . . ?

(SNOBSON, *who has been writing but stopping occasionally to listen, now gives vent to a demonic laugh.*)

TRUEMAN. (*Facing* TIFFANY.) Hey? What's that? Another of those deuced ill-sounding city laughs! (*Turns and sees* SNOBSON.) Who's this perched up on the stool of repentance—eh, Antony?

SNOBSON. (*To audience.*) The old boy has missed his text there—*that's* the stool of repentance old Tiff is sitting on!

TIFFANY. One of my clerks—my confidential clerk. (*Cross to* D.R. *desk.*)

TRUEMAN. Confidential! (TRUEMAN *and* SNOBSON *swing their heads simultaneously toward each other, then swing away.*) Why he looks for all the world like a spy, (*Head bus. repeated.*) —the most inquisitorial hang-dog face . . . (*Repeat head bus.*) Ugh! the sight of him makes my blood run cold. (*Crosses* R. *to* TIFFANY, *takes his arm.*) Come, let us talk over matters where this critter can't give us the benefit of his opinion! (*They cross to* R.E.) Antony, the next time you choose a confidential clerk, take one that carries his credentials in his

face—those in his pocket are not worth much without!
(*Exeunt* R. 2 E.)

SNOBSON. (*Jumps from his stool and crosses to desk.*)
The old prig has got the tin, or Tiff would never be so
civil! ALL RIGHT! Tiff will work every shiner into the
concern—all the better for me! (*Crosses* L. *putting on
coat and hat.*) Now I'll go and make love to Seraphina.
The old woman needn't try to knock me down with any
of her French lingo! (*Crossing down.*) Six months from
today if I ain't driving my two-footmen tandem down
Broadway—and as fashionable as Mrs. Tiffany herself,
then I ain't the trump I thought I was! That's all.
(*Looks at his watch.*) Bless me! Eleven o'clock and I
haven't had my julep yet! Joe Snobson, I'm ashamed of
you! (*Exits* C.)

CURTAIN

END SCENE 1

MUSICAL SELECTION: "Camptown Races" *sung by*
ZEKE *before Olco Curtain.*

(ZEKE *enters* L., *carrying a slide trombone. During intro.
he smiles, shows trombone to audience, fits his lips
to it, moves the slide etc. as if about to play, then
suddenly stops bus. and sings.*)
De Camptown ladies sing dis song,
Doo-dah, doo-dah,
De Camptown racetrack five miles long,
All the doo-dah day.
Come down here with my hat caved in,
Doo-dah, doo-dah,
Go back home wid a pocket full o' tin,
All the doo-dah day.

Gwine to run all night,
Gwine to run all day,
Bet mah money on a bob-tail nag,
Somebody bet on de bay.

(*Intro. continues as* ZEKE *exits* L. *Re-enters with trombone and music-stand. Sets it up with elaborate care, almost plays, then:*)

> Old muley cow come onto de track,
> Doo-dah, doo-dah;
> Bob-tail nag fling him over his back,
> All the doo-dah day,
> Flyin' along like a railroad car,
> Doo-dah, doo-dah,
> Runnin' a race wid a shootin' star,
> All the doo-dah day.
>
> Gwine to run all night, etc. (*Chorus.*)

(ZEKE *exits again, returning immediately with a piece of sheet music. Elaborate business, gets set to play, then stops and sings:*)

> See 'em runnin' a ten-mile heat,
> Doo-dah, doo-dah,
> Around the track and then repeat,
> All the doo-dah day.
> Bet my money on a bob-tail nag,
> Doo-dah, doo-dah,
> Carry mah money in an old tow bag,
> All the doo-dah day.
>
> Gwine to run all night, etc. (*Chorus.*)

(*On very last note of the song,* ZEKE [*or someone in the the wings*] *blows a beautiful, clear note. Quick exit, carrying all the props off.*)

ACT TWO

SCENE 2

The interior of a beautiful conservatory. Set consists of an elaborate painted drop only. GERTRUDE *discovered* U.R. *watering the "flowers" painted on the drop.* COLONEL HOWARD *stands on her Right, regarding her.*

HOWARD. I am afraid you lead a sad life here, Miss Gertrude?

GERTRUDE. (*Turning to him, gaily.*) What! Amongst the flowers! (*Turns away and resumes bus.*)

HOWARD. No, amongst the thistles, (*Indicating* L.) with which Mrs. Tiffany surrounds you; the tempests, which her temper raises.

GERTRUDE. (*Turning towards him again.*) They never harm me. (*Pointing to flowers above her.*) Flowers and herbs are excellent tutors. I learn prudence from the reed, (*Putting can down.*) and bend until the storm has passed over me! (*Crosses down a little.*)

HOWARD. (*Dead-pan.*) Admirable philosophy! But still this frigid atmosphere of fashion must be uncongenial to you? Accustomed to the pleasant companionship of your kind friends in Geneva, New York, (*Pointing to* R. *with a stiff gesture.*) surely you must regret this cold exchange? (*Crosses down to level with her.*)

GERTRUDE. Do you think so? Do you think I could possibly prefer a ramble in the woods to a promenade on Broadway? A wreath of scented wild flowers to a bouquet of these sickly exotics? The odor of new-mown hay (*Crossing him to* R.) to the heated air of this crowded conservatory? (*Turns* L. *to him.*) Or can you imagine that I could enjoy the quiet conversation of my Geneva friends more than the edifying chit-chat of a fashionable drawing-room. (*She smiles; he frowns.*) But I see you think me totally destitute of taste?

HOWARD. (*Pronouncing the words very distinctly.*) You have a merry spirit to jest thus at your grievances!

GERTRUDE. (*Crossing L. to him.*) I have my *mania*— as some wise person declares all mankind have—and mine is a love of independence! In Geneva, N.Y., my wants were supplied by two kind old maiden ladies, upon whom I know not that I have any claim. (*With spirit.*) I had abilities, and desired to use them. I came here at my own request; for here I am no longer *dependent!* (*Crossing above him to L. Gets watering-can and resumes business.*) *Voila tout,* as Mrs. Tiffany would say!

HOWARD. (*Crossing up to her R.*) Believe me, I appreciate the confidence you repose in me!

GERTRUDE. (*Turning to him.*) Confidence! Truly, Colonel Howard, the *confidence* is entirely on your part, in supposing that I confide that which I have no reason to conceal! (*Steps down so that he may not see her merry, nay, her mischievous smile.*) I think I informed you that Mrs. Tiffany received visitors only on her reception day. She is therefore not prepared to see you. (*She puts down the watering-can.*) Zeke—Oh! I beg his pardon—Adolph, made some mistake in admitting you.

HOWARD. Nay, Gertrude, it was not Mrs. Tiffany, nor Miss Tiffany, whom I came to see. It was— (*Steps near her.*) It was . . .

GERTRUDE. (*Turning to him.*) The conservatory, perhaps? I will leave you to examine the flowers at leisure! (*She crosses him to R.C.*)

HOWARD. (*A step R.*) Gertrude, listen to me. (*She stops R. He crosses down a few steps, aside.*) If I only dared to give utterance to what is hovering upon my lips!

MUSICAL SELECTION: "Call Me Pet Names"

(*There is a four-bar Introduction. On the first bar, HOWARD looks at GERTRUDE; on the second he crosses to her; on the third they clasp hands, cross down and hold; on the fourth they sing.*)

BOTH. (*Looking front.*)
Call me pet names, dearest, call me a bird,
GERTRUDE.
That flies to thy heart at one cherishing word;
That folds its wild wings there,
Ne'er dree-heem-ing of flight,
That tenderly sings there in loving delight.
Oh, my sad heart is pining for one fond word,
Call me pet names, dearest, call me a bird.

(HOWARD *backs a step, holding her hand.*)

HOWARD.
Call me pet names, dearest, call me a star, (*Points
heavenward.*)
Whose smiles beaming welcome thou feelst from afar;
Whose light is the clearest, the truest to thee,
When the night time of sorrow steals over life's sea,

(*Hand gesture describing waves.*)

Oh, trust thy rich bark, where its warm rays are,
Call me pet names, dearest, call me a star.

(HOWARD *to level with her, puts his arm round her waist,
and she holds his free hand.*)

DUET.
Call me sweet names, darling, call me thine own.
Speak to me always in love's low tone.
Let not thy look nor thy voice grow cold;
Let my fond worship thy being enfold.
Love me forever and love me alone,—
Call me pet names, darling, call me thine own.

(*They return to Upstage positions to continue dialogue.*)

HOWARD. Gertrude!

GERTRUDE. (*Turning to him.*) Colonel Howard!

HOWARD. Gertrude, I must . . . (*He kneels.*) I must . . .

GERTRUDE. (*Pulling him to his feet.*) Yes, indeed you *must*, must leave me! (*Crosses to* L. *of* HOWARD.) I think I hear somebody coming—Mrs. Tiffany would not be well pleased to find you here—pray, pray leave me—that door will lead you to the street. (*She hustles him off* R. 2 E. *as he protests. She sighs, returns to* U.L., *gets watering-can, resumes business, pauses, looks at audience, comes down centre.*) What a strange being is man! Why should he hesitate to say—nay, why shoul·' I prevent his saying, that which I would most delight to hear? Truly man *is* strange—but woman is quite as incomprehensible! (*She crosses up to drop,* R. *side and uses the watering-can.*)

COUNT. (*Entering* L. 2 E., *sticks his head in behind the wing and says, "Ah-hah!" Then crosses to* D.L.C.) There she is, the bewitching little creature! Mrs. Tiffany and her daughter are out of earshot. I caught a glimpse of their feathers floating down Broadway, not ten minutes ago. Now for an engagement with this captivating little piece of prudery! (*He crosses close to* GERTRUDE'S L. *as she faces away, is about to whisper in her ear, but decides to cross down a step again to address audience.*) 'Pon my honor, I'm almost afraid she won't resist a *Count* long enough to give value to the conquest. (*He crosses to her* R. *again.*) Ma belle petite, were you gathering roses for me?

GERTRUDE. (*Starts upon first perceiving him, but instantly recovers her self-possession.*) The roses here, Sir, are carefully guarded with thorns. If you have the right to gather, pluck for yourself! (*She crosses down, he holds her arm and crosses down with her.*)

COUNT. Sharp as ever, little Gertrude! But now that we are alone, throw off this frigidity, and be at your ease. (*His head over her* L. *shoulder.*)

GERTRUDE. (*Raising her shoulder so that it catches him a blow under the chin.*) Permit me to *be alone*, Sir, that I *may* be at my ease! (GERTRUDE *crosses him to* L.C.)

COUNT. Very good, *ma belle,* well said! (*Applauding her with his hands.*) Never yield too soon, even to a *title!* (*Changing his manner.*) But, as the old girl may find her way back before long, we may as well come to particulars at once. (*Rubbing his eye-glass unconcernedly with his handkerchief.*) I love you, but that you know already. Before long I shall make Mademoiselle Seraphina my wife, and, of course, *you* shall remain in the family. (*Leering, he crosses close to her.*)

GERTRUDE. (*Indignantly.*) Sir!

COUNT. 'Pon my honor you shall! In France we arrange these little matters without difficulty!

GERTRUDE. But I am an *American,* Sir! Your conduct proves that you are not one! (*She starts to exit* L., *he catches her arm.*)

COUNT. Don't run away, my immaculate *petite Americaine!* Demme, you've quite overlooked my condescension—the difference in our stations—you a species of upper servant—an orphan—no friends . . .

(*Enter* TRUEMAN R. *unperceived. He pretends to conceal himself behind some painted shrubbery.*)

GERTRUDE. And therefore more entitled to the respect and protection of every *true gentleman!* Had you been one you would not have insulted me!

COUNT. (*Running his hand up and down her arm.*) My charming little orator, patriotism and declamation become you particularly. (*He puts his lips to her neck as she throws her head back in helpless fashion.*) I feel quite tempted to taste . . .

TRUEMAN. (*Who has quietly approached, now grabs the* COUNT *and throws him across to the* R.) . . . An American hickory switch! (*Stricking him with his cane.*) Well, how do you like it?

COUNT. (*On one knee, to the front.*) Old matter-of-fact! (*To* TRUEMAN.) Sir, how dare you?

TRUEMAN. My stick has answered that question!

GERTRUDE. Oh! Now I am quite safe!

TRUEMAN. Safe! Not a bit safer than before! All women would be safe, if they knew how virtue became them! As for you, Mr. Count, what have you to say for yourself? Come, speak out! (*Crossing a step toward the* COUNT.)

COUNT. Sir,—aw—aw—you don't understand these matters. (*Crossing down 2 steps.*)

TRUEMAN. That's a fact! Not having had *your* experience, I don't believe I *do* understand them!

COUNT. A piece of pleasantry—a mere joke—

TRUEMAN. A joke, was it! I'll teach you how we natives joke with a puppy who don't respect an honest woman! (*He pushes* COUNT *to his knees at* D.R.C.)

COUNT. Oh! Demme—you old ruffian! Let me go!

TRUEMAN. (*Raising his stick as* GERTRUDE *backs up* L. *a few steps in terror.*) A piece of pleasantry, eh? A mere joke! (*The* COUNT *cringes as* MRS. TIFFANY *enters* L. 2 E., *rushing in to* L. *of* TRUEMAN.)

MRS. TIFFANY. What *is* the matter? I am perfectly *abiné* with terror. Mr. Trueman, what has happened?

TRUEMAN. Oh, we've only been joking! (COUNT *rises and crosses* 1 D.R.)

MRS. TIFFANY. (*Crossing* TRUEMAN *to* L. *of* COUNT.) My dear Count, I didn't expect to find you here—how kind of you!

TRUEMAN. Your *dear* Count has been showing his kindness in a very *foreign* manner. Too *foreign,* I think, for an *unfashionable native!* What do you think of a puppy who insults an innocent girl all in the way of kindness? (*On the line he extends his* L. *hand toward* GERTRUDE, *who dutifully comes to him. He puts his arm around her protectively.*) This Count of yours—this importation of . . .

COUNT. My dear Madam! (MRS. TIFFANY *crosses closer to* COUNT.) Demme, permit me to explain. It would be unbecoming, demme,—aw—particularly unbecoming for you to pay any attention (*Crossing to* L. *of*

Mrs. Tiffany.) to this ignorant person. Anything he says . . . a man of my standing . . . aw . . . the truth is, Madam . . .

Trueman. Let us have the truth by all means, if only for novelty's sake!

Count. (*Turns his back on* Trueman, *crosses to* Mrs. Tiffany.) You see, Madam, hoping to obtain a few moments' private conversation with *Miss Seraphina* . . . (Gertrude *gasps in shocked surprise and crosses down a few steps.*) . . . with Miss *Seraphina* I say . . . and . . . aw . . . knowing her passion for flowers, I found my way to your very tasteful and *recherché* conservatory. (*As he says this he crosses in a circle up to drop and smells one of the painted flowers.*) *Very* beautifully arranged. Here I encountered this young person. (*Crosses to* L. *of* Mrs. Tiffany.) She was inclined to be talkative; and I indulged her with . . . aw . . . demme . . . a few *commonplaces!* Mere harmless *badinage* . . . on *my* part. (*Takes* Mrs. Tiffany's *arm and draws her further to* R.) You, Madam, you . . . so conversant with our European manners . . . you are aware that when a man of fashion . . . that is, when a woman . . . a man is bound . . . amongst noblemen, you know . . .

Mrs. Tiffany. I comprehend you perfectly, Count . . . *parfittement.*

Count. (*Aside.*) 'Pon my honor that's very obliging of her.

Mrs. Tiffany. I am shocked at the plebeian forwardness of this conceited girl!

Trueman. (*Crossing* R. *a step.*) Did you ever keep a reckoning of the lies you tell in an hour?

Mrs. Tiffany. (*A step* L.) Mr. Trueman, I blush for you!

Trueman. Don't do that. . . . You have no blushes to spare. (*Crosses* U.L. 2.)

Mrs. Tiffany. It is a man of rank whom you are addressing, Sir!

Trueman. A rank villain, Mrs. Antony Tiffany!

(*Crossing* Gertrude *to* D.L.) *A rich one* he would be, had he as much *gold* as *brass!*

Mrs. Tiffany. Pray, pardon him, Count, he knows nothing of the *how ton.*

Count. Demme, he's beneath my notice. (*Crossing toward* Truman.) I tell you what, old fellow . . . (Trueman *raises his stick,* Count *retreats a step, then comes forward for aside.*) The very sight of him discomposes me . . . aw . . . I feel quite uncomfortable. (*Crosses up to* L. *of* Mrs. Tiffany *and leads her up to* R. 2 E.) Let us join your charming daughter, Madame. (*Turns back.*) I can't do you the honor to shoot you, Sir . . . you are beneath me . . . a nobleman can't fight a commoner! Good-bye, old Truepenny! I . . . aw . . . I'm insensible to your insolence! (*Exeunt* Count *and* Mrs. Tiffany R. 2 E.)

Trueman. (*Following them up to the exit.*) You won't be insensible to a cow hide in spite of your nobility! (*Crossing* L. 2.) The next time he practices his foreign fashions on you, Gertrude, you'll see how I'll wake up his sensibilities!

Gertrude. (*Joining him at* R.C.) I do not know what I should have done without you, Sir. (*MUSIC CUE— "Hearts and Flowers."*)

Trueman. Yes, you do . . . you know you would have done well enough! Never tell a lie, girl! Not even for the sake of pleasing an old man. When you open your lips let your heart speak. Let your face be the looking-glass of your soul . . . your heart its clock . . . while your tongue rings the hours! But the glass must be clear, the clock true, and then there's no fear but the tongue will do its duty in a woman's head!

Gertrude. You are very good, Sir!

Trueman. That's as it may be! (*He looks at her fondly, then crosses down a step. Aside.*) How my heart warms towards her! (*Steps up.*) Gertrude, I hear that you have no mother!

Gertrude. Ah! no, Sir . . . I often wish I had. (*Crosses down to* C. *line.*)

TRUEMAN. So do I! (*Aside, and with much emotion.*) Heaven knows, so do I! (*Crosses to her* R.) And you have no father, Gertrude?

GERTRUDE. (*Turning Downstage.*) No, Sir. I often wish I had!

TRUEMAN. (*Rather violently.*) Don't do that, girl, don't do that! Wish you had a mother . . . but never wish that you had a father again! Perhaps the one you had did not deserve such a child! (*MUSIC Out.*)

(*Enter* PRUDENCE U.R.E. *Crosses* D.R.)

PRUDENCE. Seraphina is looking for you, Gertrude.

GERTRUDE. (*Crossing toward* R. 2 E.) I will go to her. (*Turns back at entrance.*) Mr. Trueman, you will not permit me to thank you, but you cannot prevent my gratitude! (*Curtsies and exits* R. 2 E.)

TRUEMAN. (*Wipes his eyes, looks to front, gestures* R.) If falsehood harbors there, I'll give up searching after truth! (*Crosses up to drop at* C. *Looks at flowers.*)

PRUDENCE. (*Trying to attract* TRUEMAN'S *attention.*) Ahem! What a nice old man he is, to be sure! Ahem!! (*Aside.*) I wish he would say something! (TRUEMAN *crosses toward* R. *at back.* PRUDENCE *circles up to his* L., *close to him.*) Don't mind *me*, Mr. Trueman!

TRUEMAN. Mind you? Oh, don't be afraid . . . I wasn't minding you. (*Crossing further to* R.) Nobody seems to mind you much! (*Looks at flowers.*)

PRUDENCE. (*Following him.*) Very pretty flowers, ain't they? Gertrude takes care of them. (*Turns down a step or two.*)

TRUEMAN. (*Turning in.*) Gertrude? So I hear. (*Crossing to her* R.) I suppose you can tell me now who this Gertrude . . . er . . .

PRUDENCE. Who she's in love with? *I knew* you were going to ask me that! I can tell you all about it! Gertrude —she's in love with—Mr. Twinkle! And he's in love with her. And Seraphina, she's in love with Count Jolly . . . Whatchamacallit. But Count Jolly don't take to her at all! But Colonel Howard . . . he's the man . . . he's desperate about her! (*Crosses* R. *to* R.C., *crossing* TRUE-MAN.)

TRUEMAN. Why you feminine newspaper! Howard in love with that quintessence of affectation! Howard, the only frank, straightforward fellow that I've met since . . . I'll tell him my mind on the subject! And Gertrude hunting for happiness in a rhyming dictionary! (*Crossing 2* L.) The girl's a bigger fool than I took her for!

PRUDENCE. So she is. You see I know all about them!

TRUEMAN. Yes, I see. You've a wonderful knowledge— wonderful—of *other people's concerns!* It may do here, but in the county of Catteraugus you'd get the name of a great *busy-body*. But perhaps you know that, too?

PRUDENCE. (*Crossing to him.*) Oh! I always know what's coming. I feel it beforehand all over me. I felt right off that you were a bachelor!

TRUEMAN. Did you now? You were sure of it? (PRU-DENCE *nods her head several times, delightedly.*) Then you felt wrong! A bachelor and a widower are not the same thing! (*Crosses to* D.L.C.)

PRUDENCE. Oh! but it all amounts to the same thing— a widower's as good as a bachelor any day! And I know all about you! (*Coyly fingering her shawl.*) I knew—I knew you were for getting married soon! (*Nudging him with her elbow.*)

TRUEMAN. Well, I can't say that I know any such thing! you know! (*Nudging her in return.*)

PRUDENCE. For my part I like farmers. And I know all about setting hens and turkeys, and feeding chickens and laying eggs, and all that sort of thing! (*Crosses a step* R.)

TRUEMAN. (*Aside.*) May I be shot if mistress news-paper isn't putting in an advertisement for herself! This is your city mode of courting, I suppose, ha, ha, ha!

PRUDENCE. (*Crossing to his* R.) I've been west a little; but I never was in the county of Catteraugus myself.

TRUEMAN. Oh, you were not? And you have taken a particular fancy to go there, eh?

PRUDENCE. (*Smiling coyly to front.*) Perhaps I shouldn't object . . .

TRUEMAN. Oh!—Ah!—So I suppose. Now pay attention to what I'm going to say, for it is a matter of great importance to yourself.

PRUDENCE. (*Delightedly, aside.*) It's coming! I know what he's going to say! (*To him.*) Yes, Mr. Trueman?

TRUEMAN. The next time you want to tie a man to your apronstrings, pick out one that don't come from the county of Catteraugus—for greenhorns are scarce in those parts, and modest women plenty. (*Exits* L. 2 E.)

PRUDENCE. (*To front.*) Now who would have thought he was going to say that! But I won't give him up yet— I won't give him up. (*Going after him.*) Mr. Trueman! Mr. Trueman! (*Exits* L. 2 E.)

CURTAIN

MUSICAL SELECTION: "Croquet," MR. TWINKLE. *Sung before the Curtain.*

(TWINKLE *enters* R. *Attitude: serious, pompous, most circumspect. Crosses to* C. *Always returns to straight stiff pose, hands primly folded.*)

Out on the lawn in the evening gray,
Went Willie and Kate. I said, "Which way?"
And they both replied, "Croquet, Croquet."
Of mallets and balls the usual display,
The hoops all stood in arch array,
And I said to myself,
"Soon we'll see Croquet. We'll see Croquet!"

But the mallets and balls unheeded lay,
And the youth and the maid side by side sat they.
And I thought to myself—"Is that Croquet?"
I saw the scamp, it was bright as day,

Put him arm 'round her waist in a loving way;
And he squeezed her hand . . .
Was that Croquet? Was that Croquet?

(*Growing into operatic pose and voice.*)

While the red rover rolled all forgotten away,
He whisp'red all that a lover should say,
And he kissed her lips. . . . What a queer Croquet!

(*Crosses to* R. *Holds at exit. Crescendo.*)

Silent they sat 'neath the moon of May,
But I knew by her blushes she said not nay;
And I thought in my heart,
Now that's Croquet! Now that's Croquet! (*Exit* R.)

(*Piano vamps.* TWINKLE *re-appears for encore, sings
one note, PIANO stops. He exits in high dudgeon.*)

ACT THREE

SCENE 1

MRS. TIFFANY'S *Parlor. Enter* MRS. TIFFANY R. 3 E. *followed closely by* MR. TIFFANY.

TIFFANY. Your extravagance will ruin me, Mrs. Tiffany!

MRS. TIFFANY. (*At* R.C.) And your stinginess will ruin me, Mr. Tiffany. (*Crossing to* L. *of ottoman.*) It is totally and *toot a fate* impossible to convince you of the necessity of *keeping up appearances.*

TIFFANY. (*Following to her* R.) It was for *fashion's* sake that you insisted upon my buying this expensive house. (*She crosses up around ottoman to* U.C. *He follows.*) It was for *fashion's* sake that you ran me into debt. (*She crosses to* D.C. *He follows.*) It was for *fashion's* sake that you built that ruinous conservatory!

MRS. TIFFANY. (*Crossing to chair and sitting.*) Mr. Tiffany, you are insufferably *American* in your grovelling ideas! And pray, what was the occasion of these very *mal-ap-pro-pos* remarks? Merely because I asked you for a paltry fifty dollars to purchase a new style of headdress, a *bijou* of an article just introduced from France. (*Fans herself.*)

TIFFANY. (*Crossing to* L. *of her chair.*) Time was, Mrs. Tiffany, when you manufactured your own French headdresses. And all you knew about France, or French either, was what you spelt out at the bottom of your fashion-plates—but now you have grown so fashionable, forsooth, that you have forgotten how to speak your mother tongue! (*Crosses* D.L. 2.)

MRS. TIFFANY. (*Rising.*) Mr. Tiffany, Mr. Tiffany! Nothing is more positively vulgarian—more unaristocratic, than any allusion to the past. (*Crossing towards him.*)

TIFFANY. Mrs. Tiffany . . . !

MRS. TIFFANY. Mr. Tiffany! I desire you to purchase Count d'Orsay's "Science of Etiquette" and learn how to conduct yourself—especially before you appear at the grand ball which I shall give on Friday! (*She sweeps past him to* D.L.C.)

TIFFANY. (U.C.) Confound your balls, Madam; they make *footballs* of my money, while you dance away all that I am worth! A pretty time to give a ball . . . (*Crossing to her* R. *at* D.L.C.) when you know that I am on the very brink of bankruptcy!

MRS. TIFFANY. All the more reason that no-one should suspect your circumstances. Why, you would lose all your credit at once. (TIFFANY *groans and crosses to* U.C.) Just at this crisis a ball is absolutely necessary to save your reputation!

TIFFANY. But, Mrs. Tiff . . .

MRS. TIFFANY. Quiet, Sir! (*Seats herself on ottoman.*) I'm sure I've done all I could to gratify you. There is that vulgar old torment, Trueman. Haven't I been very civil to him?

TIFFANY. (*Crossing to her* R.) Civil to his *wealth*, Mrs. Tiffany! I told you he was a rich old farmer, the early friend of my father, my own benefactor, and that he might assist me in my present embarrassment. Your civility was *bought,* and like most of your *own* purchases has yet to be *paid* for. (*Crosses down 2.*)

MRS. TIFFANY. Mr. Trueman has been insupportably indecorous. He has insulted Count Jollymayter in the most outrageous manner. If the Count was not so deeply interested, so *abimé* with Seraphina, I am sure he would never honor us by his visits again! (*Fans herself furiously.*)

TIFFANY. So much the better. (*Crosses to her* R.) He shall never marry my daughter!—I am resolved on that!

MRS. TIFFANY. (*Rising.*) Nonsense, Mr. Tiffany. The Count, the intimate friend of all the dukes and lords in Europe—not marry my daughter! (*Crossing him to chair.*) Mr. Tiffany, you are out of your senses! (*Sits chair.*)

TIFFANY. That would not be very wonderful considering how many years I have been united to you, my dear.

MRS. TIFFANY. Mr. Tiffany, he is a man of fashion . . .

TIFFANY. Fashion makes fools, but cannot *feed* them. (*Crossing to her* L.) Oh! that reminds me—since you are bent on ruining me by this ball, I desire that you will send an invitation to my confidential clerk, Mr. Joseph Snobson.

MRS. TIFFANY. (*Rising.*) Mr. Snobson! Was there ever such an *you-nick* demand! Mr. Snobson would cut a pretty figure amongst my fashionable friends! (*Crossing down.*) I shall do no such thing, Mr. Tiffany.

TIFFANY. (*Crossing close to her* L.) Then, Madam, the ball shall not take place. Have I not told you I am in the power of this man? There are circumstances that make it essential that you should be civil to Mr. Snobson! Not you merely, but Seraphina also. He is a more appropriate match for her than your foreign favorite.

MRS. TIFFANY. A match for Seraphina indeed! Mr. Tiffany, you are determined to make a *fow pass.*

TIFFANY. (*Crosses* R. *to* R. *of chair.*) Mr. Snobson intends calling this morning.

MRS. TIFFANY. But, Mr. Tiffany, this is not reception day. (*Crossing* U.C.) My drawing rooms are in the most terrible disorder.

TIFFANY. Mr. Snobson is not particular. He must be admitted.

ZEKE. (*Entering* L. 2 E.) Mr. Snobson.

SNOBSON. (*Enter* L. 2 E. *and crosses to* MRS. TIFFANY'S L.) How d'ye do, Marm? How are you? (*Bows toward* MR. TIFFANY.) Mr. Tiffany, your most!

MRS. TIFFANY. (*Formally.*) *Bung jure. Comment vow porte vow, Monsur Snobson?*

SNOBSON. Oh, to be sure—very good of you—fine day.

MRS. TIFFANY. (*Pointing to the chair, with great dignity.*) *Sassoyez vow, Monsur Snobson.*

SNOBSON. (*Aside.*) I wonder what she's driving at? I

ain't up to the fashionable lingo yet! Eh? What? (*Cupping his ear.*) Speak a little louder, Marm.

MRS. TIFFANY. What ignorance! (*Sweeps up to* L. *of fireplace* U.C.)

TIFFANY. I presume Mrs. Tiffany means that you are to take a seat.

SNOBSON. Ex-actly—very obligin' of her—so I will. (*Crosses to* TIFFANY.) No ceremony amongst friends, you know—and likely to be nearer—you understand? O.K., all correct. (*Sits chair.*) How *is* Seraphina?

MRS. TIFFANY. Miss Tiffany is not visible this morning.

SNOBSON. (*Jumping up.*) Not visible! (*Crosses* L. *a step.*) I suppose that's the English for can't see her! (*Crosses to* TIFFANY D.R.C.) Mr. Tiffany, Sir—what am I to understand by this *de-fal-ca-tion*, Sir? I expected your word to be as good as your bond—beg pardon, Sir —I mean better—considerably better—no humbug about it, Sir.

TIFFANY. (*Crossing up to bellpull* R. *of fireplace* C.) Have patience, Mr. Snobson. (*Rings bell.* MRS. TIFFANY *crosses to* L. *of ottoman going above it.* ZEKE *enters* L. 2 E.)

ZEKE. Yassuh, boss! (*Crosses to* R. *of ottoman.*)

TIFFANY. Zeke, desire my daughter to come here. (*Indicate Off* R.)

ZEKE. Yassuh, boss. (*Starts* R. *but* MRS. TIFFANY *crosses to his* L. *and halts him.*)

MRS. TIFFANY. Adolph—I say—Adolph . . .

(ZEKE, *between them, straightens up and assumes foppish airs. Turns to* MRS. TIFFANY.)

TIFFANY. (*Commandingly.*) Zeke!

ZEKE. Don't know any such person, boss.

TIFFANY. Do as I bid you instantly, or off with your livery and quit the house!

ZEKE. Wheugh! I'se all dismission! (*Exits quickly* R. 3 E.)

MRS. TIFFANY. (*Calling after him.*) Adolph! Adolph! (*Sits ottoman.*)

SNOBSON. (*Crosses to* D.R.C. *as* TIFFANY *crosses up to* R. *side fireplace. Aside.*) I brought the old boy to his bearings, didn't I though! Pull that string and he's sure to work right. (*Crosses to* R. *of* MRS. TIFFANY.) Don't make any stranger of me, Marm. I'm quite at home. If you've got any odd jobs to do about the house, I won't miss you. I'll amuse myself with Seraphina when she comes—we'll get along very cosily by ourselves.

MRS. TIFFANY. (*Rising.*) Permit me to inform you, Mr. Snobson, that a French mother never leaves her daughter alone with a young man. She knows your sex too well for that. (*Crosses to* D.L.)

SNOBSON. Very dis-obligin' of her—but as we're none French . . .

MRS. TIFFANY. (*Turning towards him.*) You have yet to learn, Mr. Snobson, that the American *ee-light,* the aristocracy, the *how ton,* as a matter of conscience scrupulously follow the foreign fashions.

SNOBSON. Not when they are foreign to their interests, Marm. For instance . . . (*Enter* SERAPHINA R. 3 E.) Ah, there you are at last, eh Miss? (*She stops below chair.* SNOBSON *crosses directly to her.*) How d'ye do? Ma said you weren't visible. Managed to get a peep at her, eh, Mr. Tiffany?

SERAPHINA. (*Crosses down a step, coquettishly.*) I heard you were here, Mr. Snobson, and came without even arranging my toilette; you will excuse my negligence?

SNOBSON. (*Licking his lips.*) Of everything but *me,* Miss.

SERAPHINA. (*Flirtatiously.*) I shall never have to ask your pardon for *that,* Mr. Snobson.

MRS. TIFFANY. (*Alarmed.*) Seraphina—child—really . . . (*She starts to cross towards them, but* MR. TIFFANY *comes down and intercepts her.*)

TIFFANY. (*Pointing* L.) Walk this way, Madam, if you

please. (*Aside.*) To see that she fancies this surly fellow takes a weight from my heart.

MRS. TIFFANY. Mr. Tiffany, it is highly improper and not at all *distingué* to leave a young girl . . .

(*Enter* ZEKE L. 2 E.)

ZEKE. Mr. Count Jolly-made-her! (MR. TIFFANY *crosses up to* R. *of ottoman.*)

MRS. TIFFANY. Good gracious! The Count— Oh, dear! (*Crosses to* L. *of* SNOBSON.) Seraphina! (SERAPHINA *crosses down 1.*) Run and change your dress,—no there's not time! (*Turns* L.) A-dolph, admit him! (ZEKE *exits* L. 2 E.) Mr. Snobson, get out of the way, will you? (*Pushes him* D.R. *He lands* R. *of* SERAPHINA. MR. TIFFANY *sits* L. *side ottoman. She crosses toward him.*) Mr. Tiffany, what are you doing home at this hour?

ZEKE. (*Entering* L. 2 E.) Count Jolly-made-her! (COUNT *enters, crosses directly to* L. *of* MRS. TIFFANY.)

MRS. TIFFANY. My dear Count! (*They freeze for* ZEKE'S *aside.*)

ZEKE. (*At* L. 2 E.) Dat's de genuine article ob a gemman! (*Exits.*)

MRS. TIFFANY. Overjoyed!

COUNT. Flattered myself you'd be glad to see me, Madam—knew it was not your *jour de reception.* (*Kisses her hand.*)

MRS. TIFFANY. But for you, Count, all days . . .

COUNT. I thought so. (*Sees* SERAPHINA.) Ah, Miss Tiffany! (*Crosses to her as* TIFFANY *rises and crosses* D.L. *a step.*) On my honor, you're looking beautiful! (*Kisses her hand, wrist, etc.*)

SERAPHINA. Count, flattery from you . . .

SNOBSON. (*On her* R.) What? Eh? What's that you say? (COUNT *turns* L.)

SERAPHINA. Nothing but what etiquette requires.

COUNT. (*Regards* MR. TIFFANY *through his eye-glass, crosses* L. *to* R. *of* TIFFANY.) Your worthy papa, I believe? Sir, your most obedient. (COUNT *sits on otto-man.*)

SNOBSON. (*Crossing to* R. *of* MRS. TIFFANY *at* C.) Introduce me, will you? I never knew a Count in all my life . . . what a strange looking animal!

MRS. TIFFANY. Mr. Snobson, it is not the fashion to introduce in France!

SNOBSON. But, Marm, we're in America! (MRS. TIFFANY *crosses to* COUNT. *Aside.*) The woman thinks she's somewhere else than where she is—she wants to make an *alibi!*

MRS. TIFFANY. I hope we shall have the pleasure of seeing you on Friday evening, Count?

COUNT. (*Rising, as* MRS. TIFFANY *counters and* MR. TIFFANY *drops down further Left.*) Really, Madam, my invitations . . . engagements . . . so numerous . . . I can hardly answer for myself: and you Americans take offense so easily . . .

MRS. TIFFANY. But, Count, everybody expects you at our ball—you are the principal attraction . . .

SERAPHINA. Count, you *must* come!

COUNT. (*Crossing* MRS. TIFFANY *and* SNOBSON *to* L. *of* SERAPHINA.) Since you insist . . . aw . . . aw . . . there's no resisting *you*, Miss Tiffany. (COUNT *and* SERAPHINA, *conversing, cross* D.R.)

MRS. TIFFANY. (*Pulling* SNOBSON *Upstage.*) Mr. Snobson, will you walk this way? I have *such* a cactus in full bloom—remarkable flower! Mr. Tiffany, pray come! I have something particular to say . . .

TIFFANY. (*Crossing in to* L. *of ottoman.*) Then speak out, my dear. (*Aside to her.*) I thought it was highly improper just now to leave a girl with a young man?

MRS. TIFFANY. Oh, but the Count—that is different!

TIFFANY. I suppose you mean to say there's nothing of *the man* about him? (*Crosses up to back,* L. *of otto-man.*)

(*Enter* MILLINETTE L. 2 E. *with a scarf in her hand.*)

MILLINETTE. Adolph tell me he vas here. (*Crossing to* L. *of* MRS. TIFFANY.) Pardon, Madame, I bring dis scarf for Mademoiselle.

MRS. TIFFANY. Very well, Millinette. (*She engages the attention of* SNOBSON *and* TIFFANY *and they ALL cross up to above ottoman where they sit.*)

MILLINETTE. (*Crossing the* COUNT *to* L. *of* SERAPHINA, *giving him a threatening look as she goes. She arranges the scarf on* SERAPHINA'S *shoulders.*) Mademoiselle, *permettez-moi.* (*Turns* L. *to* COUNT.) *Perfide!* (*Turns* R.) If Mademoiselle vill stand *tranquille* one *petit moment.* (*Turns* SERAPHINA'S *back to* COUNT *and pretends to arrange the scarf.*) I must speak vid you today, or I tell all! You vill find me at ze foot of ze stairs ven you go. *Prend garde!*

SERAPHINA. (*Turning.*) What's that you say, Millinette?

MILLINETTE. Zis scarf make you so very beautiful, Mademoiselle. (*Crossing* L.) *Je vous salue, mes dames.* (*Curtsies and exits* L. 2 E.)

COUNT. (*To front.*) Not a moment to lose. (*Crosses to* SERAPHINA.) Miss Tiffany, I have an unpleasant, a particularly unpleasant piece of intelligence. You see, I have just received a letter from my friend, the . . . aw . . . the Earl of Airedale; the truth is, the Earl's daughter—beg you won't mention it—has distinguished me by a tender *penchant.*

SERAPHINA. I understand. And they wish you to return and marry the young lady; but surely you will not leave us, Count?

COUNT. If *you* bid me stay . . . I shouldn't have the conscience . . . I couldn't *afford* to tear myself away. (*Aside.*) I'm sure that's honest.

SERAPHINA. Oh, Count!

COUNT. (*Pressing the attack.*) Say but one word, say that you shouldn't mind being made a Countess . . . and I'll break with the Earl tomorrow.

SERAPHINA. (*Loudly.*) Count, this surprise! But don't think of leaving the country, Count. We could not pass

the time without you! I—yes—yes, Count—I do consent!
(*They fall into an embrace.*)

COUNT. (*Aside, from the embrace.*) I thought she
would! (*To her.*) Enchanted, rapture, bliss, ecstasy, and
all that sort of thing—words can't express it, but you
understand. (*Leads her Downstage a few steps.*) But
it must be kept a secret—positively it *must!* If the
rumor of our engagement were whispered abroad—the
Earl's daughter—the delicacy of the situation, aw—you
comprehend? It is even possible that our nuptials, my
charming Miss Tiffany, *our nuptials* must take place in
private!

SERAPHINA. (*Crossing up to* U.R. *of chair.*) Oh, that
is quite impossible!

COUNT. (*Crossing up to her* L.) But it's the latest
fashion abroad, the very latest!

SERAPHINA. Well, in that case . . . of course!

COUNT. Ah, I knew that would determine you. Can I
depend on your secrecy?

SERAPHINA. Oh, yes! Believe me.

SNOBSON. (*Coming forward in spite of* MRS. TIFFANY's
efforts to detain him.) Why Seraphina, haven't you a
word to throw to a dog?

TIFFANY. (D.L. *of ottoman.*) I shouldn't think she had
after wasting so many upon a puppy.

(*Enter* ZEKE L. 2 E. *wearing a three-cornered hat.*)

ZEKE. Missus, de bran' new carriage am below.

MRS. TIFFANY. (*On* R. *of ottoman.*) Show it up,—I
mean, very well, A-dolph. (ZEKE *exits.*) Count, my
daughter and I are about to take an airing in our new
voyture,—will you honor us with your company?

COUNT. (*Crossing* SNOBSON *to* R. *of* MRS. TIFFANY.)
Madam, I—I have a most *pressing* engagement. A letter
to write to the *Earl of Airedale,* who is at present resid-
ing on the *Isle of Skye.* I must bid you good morning.
(*Kisses her hand.*)

MRS. TIFFANY. (*Beaming.*) Good morning, Count. (*He exits* L. 2 E.)

SNOBSON. (*Crossing to* R. *of* MRS. TIFFANY.) *I'm* quite at leisure, Marm. Books balanced, ledger closed, nothing to do all the afternoon. I'm for you.

MRS. TIFFANY. (*Without noticing him.*) Come Seraphina, come! (*She and* SERAPHINA *cross* L. *to entrance, as* MR. TIFFANY *crosses up around ottoman and comes down on* R. *of it.*)

SNOBSON. (*Following them.*) But, Marm—I was saying, Marm, I'm quite at leisure, not a thing to do. (*Turning* R.) Have I, Mr. Tiffany?

MRS. TIFFANY. Seraphina, child—your red shawl— remember? (SERAPHINA *exits.*) Mr. Snobson, *bon swear!* (*She exits.*)

SNOBSON. Swear! (*Crossing* R. *to* C.) Mr. Tiffany, Sir, am I to be fobbed off with a *bon swear?* Dammit, I will swear!

TIFFANY. (*On his* R.) Have patience, Mr. Snobson . . . (*Indicating* L.) if you will accompany me to the counting-house . . .

SNOBSON. Don't count too much on me, Sir. I'll make up no more accounts until these are settled! I'll run down and jump into the carriage in spite of her *bon swear!* (*Exits* L. 2 E.)

TIFFANY. You'll jump into a hornet's nest if you do! (*Crosses* L.) Mr. Snobson, Mr. Snobson! (*Stops at entrance, looks at audience.*)

MUSICAL SELECTION: "I Wish I Was Single Again," MR. TIFFANY.

When I was single, oh then, oh then,
When I was single, oh then,
When I was single, my pockets did jingle,
And I wish I was single again, again;
I wish I was single again.

I married me a wife, oh then, oh then!

I married me a wife, oh then,
I married me a wife, she's the plague of my life!
And I wish I was single again, again,
I wish I was single again.

(*Crosses* R. *Speaks this verse over the music.*)

My wife, she died, (*Happily.*) Oh then, oh then!
My wife she died, oh then!
My wife she died, and then I cried,
To think I was single again, again . . .
To think I was single again!

I married another . . . (*Indicating* L.) the devil's
   grandmother,
I wish I was single again,
For when I was single, my money did jingle,
And I wish I was single again, again,
(*In high falsetto.*) And I wish I was single again! (*Exits*
R.)

(*For encore,* TIFFANY *dances on, singing, crosses* L. *with
a long side step, swinging his arms. Exits* L. *as
though he had miscalculated where the exit was.
MUSIC continues through pause.* TIFFANY *returns,
dancing to* R. *Exits* R. *Pause as MUSIC continues.*
TIFFANY *re-enters* R. *singing, he crosses* L. *at great
speed, disappears into wings* L. *After a pause there
is a loud CRASH, which builds. MUSIC continues
as though nothing had happened. Suddenly* ZEKE
enters from L. *singing, and crosses* R. *with same
dance step, exits* R. TIFFANY *then re-enters* R. *with
a bandage around his head. Dances* L. *Pauses,
breathless, leaning against* L. *wing. At end of verse,
an arm appears from Offstage, grabs him around the
neck, and pulls him off.*)

CURTAIN

ACT THREE

Scene 2

Housekeeper's Room. MILLINETTE *discovered, pretending to make bed painted on drop. Turns and sees
audience. Tiptoes to* D.C., *indicates* L.

MILLINETTE. I have set dat *bête,* Adolph, to watch
for him. He say he vould come back as soon as Madame's
voiture drive from ze door. If he not come . . . but he
vill . . . he *vill* . . . He *bien etourdi,* (*Twirling her
finger at her temple*) but he have *bon coeur!* (*She returns to her bed-making.* COUNT *enters* L. 2 E. *Crosses
to* L.C.)

COUNT. Ah! Millinette, my dear, you see what a good-
natured dog I am to fly at your bidding . . .

MILLINETTE. (*Crossing to him.*) Fly? Ah! *Trompeur!*
Vat for you fly from Paree? Vat for you leave me—and
I love you so much! (*Throws her arms around his neck,
then bethinks herself and slaps him hard; he staggers
back.*) Ven you sick—you almost die—did I not stay by
you—take care of you—and you have no one else friend?
(*Steps back.*) Vat for you leave Paree?

COUNT. Never allude to disagreeable subjects, *mon
enfant!* I was forced by uncontrollable circumstances
to fly to the land of liberty . . . (*Crosses down a step.*)

MILLINETTE. (*Following him.*) Vat you do vid all ze
money I give you? The last sou I had, did I not give
you?

COUNT. I daresay you did, *ma petite.* (*Aside.*) Wish
you'd been better supplied! Don't ask me to explain
now . . . the next time we meet . . .

MILLINETTE. But, ah! ven shall ve meet, ven? You
not deceive me, not any more!

COUNT. (*Putting his arms around her.*) Deceive you!
I'd rather deceive myself—I wish I could! (*Aside.*) I'd
persuade myself you were once more washing linen in
the Seine!

MILLINETTE. I vill tell you ven ve shall meet— On Friday night Madame give one grand ball—you come *sans doute*—zen, ven ze supper is served—de Americans t'ink of nozzing else ven ze supper come—zen you steal out of ze room, and you find me here—and you give me one grand *explanation!*

(*Enter* GERTRUDE R., *between the drop and the wing, unperceived.*)

COUNT. Friday night, while supper is serving, *parole d'honneur* I will be here—I will explain everything—my sudden departure from Paris—my—demme, my countship—everything! Now let me go . . . if any of the family should *discover us* . . .

GERTRUDE. (*Crossing to* D.R.C. *on* R. *of* MILLINETTE.) They might discover more than you think it advisable for them to know!

COUNT. (*Who has frozen in his embrace with* MILLINETTE, *now breaks the pose and looks at* GERTRUDE. *Aside.*) The devil!

MILLINETTE. *Mon dieu!* Mademoiselle Gertrude! (*Crosses to* L. *of* COUNT.)

COUNT. (*Recovering himself.*) My dear Miss Gertrude, let me explain . . . aw . . . aw . . . nothing is more natural than the situation in which you find me . . .

GERTRUDE. I am inclined to believe that, Sir!

COUNT. Now—'pon my honor, that's deuced unfair! Here is Millinette will bear witness to what I am about to say . . .

GERTRUDE. Oh, I have not the slightest doubt of that, Sir! (*Turns away.*)

COUNT. (*Struggling to be off-hand.*) You see, Millinette happened to be lady's maid in the family of—of—the Duchess Chateau D'Espagne . . . and I chanced to be a particular friend of the Duchess . . . *very particular,* I assure you! Of course I saw Millinette, and she, demme, she saw me! (*Harshly.*) Didn't you, Millinette?

MILLINETTE. Oh! Oui— (*Putting her hand on him.*) Mademoiselle, I knew him very well . . . (*Recovers herself and drops hand.*)

COUNT. Well, it is a remarkable fact that . . . being in correspondence with this very Duchess—at this very time . . .

GERTRUDE. (*Turning to him.*) That is sufficient, Sir. I am already so well acquainted with your extraordinary talents for improvisation, that I will not further tax your invention . . .

MILLINETTE. (*Crossing to her, kneels.*) Ah! Mademoiselle Gertrude, do not betray us! Have pity!

COUNT. (*Assuming an air of dignity, thunders.*) Silence, Millinette! (MILLINETTE *rises.*) My word has been doubted—the word of a nobleman! I will inform my friend, Mrs. Tiffany, of this young person's audacity. (*He takes a few steps* L. *then freezes for* GERTRUDE'S *aside.*)

GERTRUDE. (*Aside.*) His own weapons alone can foil this villain! Sir! Sir!—Count! (*At the last word the* COUNT *turns.* GERTRUDE *crosses* L. *to him.*) Perhaps, Sir, the least said about this matter the better!

COUNT. (*Delightedly.*) The least said? We won't say anything at all! (*Crosses down to* L. *of* C. *on* L. *of* GERTRUDE, *aside.*) She's coming 'round—couldn't resist me! Charming Gertrude . . .

MILLINETTE. (*Crossing to him, turns him around.*) Quoi? Vat that you say?

COUNT. (*Aside to her.*) My sweet adorable Millinette, hold your tongue, will you?

MILLINETTE. (*Aloud.*) No, I vill not! If you do so look from out your eyes at her again, I vill tell all!

COUNT. (*Comes down, aside.*) Oh, I never could manage two women at once . . . jealousy makes the dear creatures so spiteful. The only valor is in flight! (*He crosses to exit* L. 2 E. *crossing* GERTRUDE, *turns back.*) Miss Gertrude, I wish you good morning. (*Waving his fingers.*) Millinette, *mon enfant,* adieu. (*Exits* L. 2 E.)

MILLINETTE. But I have one more word to say!
(*Crossing* L.) Stop! Stop! (*Exits after him.*)

GERTRUDE. (*Comes forward to the footlights at* C.)
Friday night, while supper is serving, he is to meet
Millinette here and explain—what? This man is an impostor! His insulting me—his familiarity with Millinette
—his whole conduct—prove it. (*Crosses* R. 2.) If I tell
Mrs. Tiffany this, she will disbelieve me, and one word
may place this so-called Count on his guard. (*Crosses
down* 1.) To convince Seraphina would be equally
difficult, and her rashness and infatuation may render
her miserable for life. No! She shall be saved! (*Crosses
up to Table at* C.) I must devise some plan for opening
their eyes. (*Crosses down a step or two.*) For truly . . .
if I *cannot* invent one, I shall be the first woman who
was ever at a loss for a stratagem—especially to punish
a villain or shield a friend. (*Curtsies.*)

CURTAIN

INTERMISSION

MUSICAL SELECTION: "The Gypsy's Warning"
(MILLINETTE) *to be sung* (*in front of Act Curtain*)
before the Act begins. (*Attitude: dramatic, darkly
serious.* MILLINETTE *enters* R. *on Intro., carries
scarf.*)

Do not trust him, gentle lady,
Though his voice be low and sweet. (*Kneels.*)
Heed not him who kneels before you,
Gently pleading at thy feet. (*Rises.*)
Now thy life is in its morning,
Cloud not this, thy happy lot,
Listen to the Gypsy's Warning, (*Scarf held across fore-
head to suggest gypsy.*)
Gentle lady, trust him not.

Listen to the Gypsy's Warning,
Gentle lady, trust him not.

(*Crosses* R. *Points to lady in front row, preferably one
    with an escort.*)

Do not turn so coldly from me!
I would only guard thy youth
From his stern and with'ring power.
I would only tell thee truth.
I would shield thee from all danger, (*Points to escort.*)
Save thee from the tempter's snare, (*Winding scarf
    around throat, pulls it tight.*)
Lady, shun that dark-eyed stranger;
I have warned thee, now beware!
Lady, shun that dark-eyed stranger;
I have warned thee, now beware!

(*Crosses to back, looks fearfully* R. *and* L. *into the wings.
    Crosses down.*)

Lady, once there lived a maiden,
Pure and bright and like thee, fair.
But he wooed and wooed and won her,
Filled her gentle heart with care.
Then he heeded not her weeping,
Nor cared he her life to save.
Soon she perished, now she's sleeping,
In the cold and silent grave. (*Crosses* R.)
Soon she perished, now she's sleeping,
In the cold and silent grave! (*Exits* R., *wiping her eyes
    with scarf. MUSIC segues to waltz.*)

ACT FOUR

Scene 1

Ball Room splendidly illuminated. As the CURTAIN rises, a gay WALTZ is in full swing. The dancing-partners are as follows: Gertrude-Howard, Sera-phina-Count, Twinkle-Mrs. Tiffany, Fogg-Extra Lady, Mr. Tiffany-Extra Lady. Zeke *moves among the dancers serving punch and sand-wiches.* Snobson *lurks in background trying to catch* Seraphina's *eye.*

Count. (D.R.C. *dancing.*) Tomorrow then, tomorrow, I may salute you as my bride . . . demme, my Countess!

Seraphina. Yes, tomorrow! (*They stop dancing.*)

Snobson. (*Crossing down between them.*) You said you'd dance with me, Miss. Now take my fin, and we'll walk about and see what's going on.

(Count *raises eye-glass, taps* Snobson *on shoulder, reaches across him and retrieves* Seraphina, *dances with her to* c. *and* u.c. Snobson *follows, endeavoring to attract her attention but meets* Zeke d.l., *helps himself to a drink and stuffs some sandwiches into his pocket.*)

Snobson. Here's a treat! Get my tomorrow's luncheon out of Tiff!

Trueman. (*Entering* r. 3 e., *crosses to* d.r.c. *with* Tiffany d.r.) What a nap I've had, to be sure! (*Looks at his watch.*) Eleven o'clock, as I'm alive! Just the time when country folks are comfortably *turned in,* and here your grand *turn-out* has hardly begun! (*To* Tiffany.)

(*MUSIC stops.*)

Gertrude. (*Crossing from* u.c. *to* Trueman's l. *as*

65

HOWARD *watches from* U.C.) I was just coming to look for you, Mr. Trueman. I began to fancy that you were paying a visit to dreamland.

TRUEMAN. So, I was, child—so I was—and I saw a face—like yours—but brighter!—even brighter. (*To* TIFFANY.) It makes one feel that the world has something worth living for in it yet! Do you remember a smile like that, Antony? Ah! I see you don't. But I do—I do! (*Much moved, he crosses* GERTRUDE *to* C., *meets* HOWARD.)

HOWARD. (*Advancing.*) Good evening, Mr. Trueman. (*Offers his hand.*)

TRUEMAN. (*Heartily.*) That's right, man; give me your whole hand! When a man offers me the tips of his fingers, I know at once there's nothing in him worth seeking beyond his fingers' ends.

MRS. TIFFANY. (*Advancing from* U.R.C. *to* D.R.C., *on* R. *of* TRUEMAN. *Aside.*) I'm in such a fidget lest this vulgar old fellow should disgrace us by some of his plebeian remarks! What it is to give a ball, when one is forced to invite vulgar people! (*She crosses up to* TRUEMAN. SERAPHINA, U.L.C., *flirts with* SNOBSON *and* TWINKLE, *who is trying to read his verses to her.*) Dear me, Mr. Trueman, you are very late—quite in the fashion I declare!

TRUEMAN. Fashion! And pray what is *fashion,* madam? —To substitute etiquette for virtue—decorum for purity —manners for morals!—to affect a shame for the works of their Creator! and expend all their rapture upon the works of their tailors and dressmakers! (MR. TIFFANY *and his partner cross to* U.R.)

MRS. TIFFANY. You have the most *ow-tray* ideas, Mr. Trueman—quite rustic, and deplorably *American!* But pray walk this way. (*She leads him* L. *toward* L. 2 E., *as* SERAPHINA *and escorts steal* R. *a step or two.*)

COUNT. (*Crossing down to* L. *of* GERTRUDE *who is* D.R.) Miss Gertrude, no opportunity to speak to you before . . . in demand, you know!

GERTRUDE. (*Aside, as* HOWARD *watches fearfully from*

c.) I have no choice, I must be civil to him! What were you remarking, Sir?

COUNT. (*Overcome with desire.*) Miss Gertrude— charming Ger . . . aw . . . aw . . . (*Aside.*) I never found it so difficult to speak to a woman before!

GERTRUDE. Yes, a very charming ball—many beautiful faces here.

COUNT. Only one! . . . aw . . . one. The fact is . . . (*Draws her further* R. *but stays on her* L.)

HOWARD. (*From* C. *crosses down to footlights, aside.*) What could old Trueman have meant by saying she fancied that puppy of a Count? (*Crosses* R. *to* L. *of* COUNT, *very close to him.*) . . . this paste jewel thrust upon the little finger of society. (*Backs swiftly to* U.C. *MUSIC plays, a lively Polka.*)

COUNT. Miss Gertrude . . . aw . . . 'pon my honor, you don't understand . . . really . . . aw . . . will you dance the polka with me?

(GERTRUDE *bows and gives him her hand. All freeze as* HOWARD *advances to footlights again.*)

HOWARD. Going to dance with him, too! A few days ago she would hardly bow to him civilly. . . . Could old Trueman have had reasons for what he said? (*Again backs swiftly to* U.C.)

(*The POLKA begins, with couples as follows:* TRUEMAN-MRS. TIFFANY, SERAPHINA-SNOBSON, GERTRUDE-COUNT, TWINKLE-EXTRA LADY, FOGG-EXTRA LADY.)

PRUDENCE. (*Peeping in from* L. 2 E. *as DANCE concludes and couples move toward the back.*) I don't like dancing on Friday; something strange is always sure to happen! I'll be on the look-out.

GERTRUDE. (*Crosses to* D.L.C. *To audience:*) They are preparing the supper. Now if I can only dispose of Millinette while I unmask this insolent pretender! (*Exits* L. 2 E.)

PRUDENCE. What's that she said? It's coming!

(*Re-enter* GERTRUDE L. 2 E. *with a small basket filled with bouquets, crosses to* L. *of* MRS. TIFFANY, *draws her* D.C.)

GERTRUDE. Excuse me, Madam, I believe this is just the hour at which you ordered supper?

MRS. TIFFANY. Well, what's that to you! So you've been dancing with the Count—how dare you dance with a nobleman—*you?*

GERTRUDE. I will answer that question half an hour hence. At present I have something to propose, which I think will gratify you and please your guests. (MRS. TIFFANY *turns away.*) I have heard that at the most elegant balls in Paris, it is customary . . .

MRS. TIFFANY. (*Turning back, immediately interested.*) What? what?

GERTRUDE. It is customary to station a servant at the door (*Indicating* R.) With a basket of flowers. A bouquet is then presented to every lady as she passes out. I prepared this basket a short time ago. As the company walk in to supper, might not the flowers be distributed to advantage?

MRS. TIFFANY. How *distingué!* You are a good creature, Gertrude. There. Run and hand the *bokettes* to them yourself! (*Leads* GERTRUDE *across her to her* R. *and turns* L. *to walk to* HOWARD.)

GERTRUDE. (*Steps down. Aside.*) Caught in my own net! But, Madam! (MRS. TIFFANY *crosses* R. *to her.*) I know so little of fashion—Millinette, being French, could do it herself with so much more grace. I am sure Millinette . . .

MRS. TIFFANY. So am I. She will do it a thousand times better than you. There. Go call her! (MRS. TIFFANY *crosses* L.)

GERTRUDE. (*Starts to cross* R. *but stops and returns to* C.) But Madam! (MRS. TIFFANY *returns to her* L.)

MRS. TIFFANY. What is it now?

GERTRUDE. Pray order Millinette not to leave her station till supper is ended. As the company pass out of the supper room, she may find that some of the ladies have been overlooked.

MRS. TIFFANY. That is true. Very thoughtful of you, Gertrude. (*Takes basket.*)

GERTRUDE. (*As she exits* R. 3 E.) Millinette!

MRS. TIFFANY. (*To front.*) What a *recherché* idea!

(MILLINETTE *enters* R. 3 E. MRS. TIFFANY *crosses to her.*)

MRS. TIFFANY. Here, Millinette, take this basket. Place yourself there (L. 2 E.) and distribute these *bokettes* as the company pass out to supper; but remember not to stir from that spot until supper is over. It is a French fashion, you know!

MILLINETTE. (*Crossing to* D.R.C. *aside.*) *Mon Dieu!* zis vill ruin all! (*Crosses back to* R. *of* MRS. TIFFANY.) Madame, madame, let me tell you, madame, dat in France, in Paree, eet eez ze custom to present *les bouquets* ven everybody first come—long *before* ze supper.

MRS. TIFFANY. Dear me! Millinette, what's the difference! Besides I'd have you know that Americans always improve upon French fashions! Here, take the basket and let me see that you do it in the most *you-nick* and genteel manner. (MILLINETTE *takes the basket and, pouting, stands up of* R. 2 E. *MUSIC plays: a March.*) Aha! Supper! Come on everybody! This way! (MRS. TIFFANY *circles to* U.C. *She and* COUNT *lead the way out* R. 2 E. *with other couples following.* TIFFANY *holds* L.C. *and* TRUEMAN U.R.C. MILLINETTE *passes the bouquets to the LADIES as they exit.*)

TRUEMAN. (*Encountering* FOGG *who is hurrying off to the supper-room.*) Mr. Fogg, never mind the supper, man! Ha, ha, ha! Of course you are indifferent to suppers!

Fogg. Indifferent! suppers—oh, ah,—no, Sir—Suppers! No, no, I'm not indifferent to suppers! (*Exits* R. *2* E.)

Trueman. Ha, ha, ha! (*To* Tiffany *who crosses in to his* L.) Here's a new discovery I've made in the fashionable world! Fashion don't permit the critters to have *heads* or *hearts,* but it allows them stomachs! (*Crossing with* Tiffany *to the exit.*) So it's not fashionable to *feel,* but it's fashionable to *feed,* eh Antony? Ha, ha, ha! (*Exeunt* R. *2* E.)

Gertrude. (*Entering* R. *3* E. *followed by* Zeke. *They cross to* D.R.) Zeke, go into the supper room instantly,— whisper to Count Jolimaitre that all is ready, and that he must keep his appointment without delay. Then watch him, and as he passes out of the room, place yourself in front of Millinette in such a manner that the Count cannot see her nor she him. Be sure that they do not see each other—everything depends upon that!

Zeke. Missy, consider dat business brought to a sanitary conclusion. (*Exits* R. *2* E. *as* Gertrude *exits* L. *2* E.)

Prudence. (*Who has been listening* U.C., *now crosses to* D.C.) What can she want of the Count? I always suspected that Gertrude, because she's so merry and busy! Mr. Trueman thinks so much of her, too. I'll tell him about this! (*Crosses to* R.C.) There's something wrong, and it all comes of giving a ball on Friday! How astonished the dear old man will be when he finds out how much I know! (*Exits* R. *2* E.)

CURTAIN

MUSICAL SELECTION: "The Man Who Broke the Bank at Monte Carlo," (Count.) *Sung in front of Oleo Curtain.*

(*On introduction* Count *enters* L. *Holds* L.C.)

I've just got here to Paris
From the sunny southern shore.

I to Monte Carlo went
Just to raise my winter's rent.
Dame Fortune smiled upon me
As she'd never done before;
And I've now such lots of money,
I'm a gent.

CHORUS. (COUNT *marches* R. *twirling cane, takes off his white gloves and throws them into* R. *wing. After a moment they are thrown back on again.*)

As I walk along the Bois Boo-long
With an independent air,
You can hear the girls declare
"He must be a millionaire!"
You can hear them sigh and wish to die,
You can see them wink the other eye
At the man who broke the bank at Monte Carlo.

(*Comes down to footlights. Confidentially.*)

I stay indoors till after lunch,
And then my daily walk
To the great Triumphal Arch (*Marches* L.)
Is one grand triumphal march!
Observed by each observer
With the keenness of a hawk,
I'm a mass of money, linen, silk, and starch,
Yes, I'm a mass of money, linen, silk, and starch!

CHORUS. (*Repeated, during which he dances from backdrop to footlights, kicking over them at end of phrase.*)

I patronized the tables (*Crosses to* L.C. *pantomiming shuffling and dealing cards.*)
At the Monte Carlo hell,
Till they hadn't got a sou
For a Christian or a Jew.

So I quickly came to Paris
For the charms of Mad'moiselle
Who's the lodestone of my heart,
What can I do?
When with twenty tongues she swears
That she'll be true.

CHORUS. (*Repeated. Marches off* R. *at Exit. For encore repeats enough of Chorus to march from* R. *to exit* L. *without looking at audience. MUSIC segues to melodrama theme.*)

ACT FOUR

SCENE 2

Housekeeper's Room; dark Stage; table U.C. *with two chairs, one on each side of it. Enter* GERTRUDE *from* L. *carrying a lighted candle, crosses to* D.L. *of table.*

GERTRUDE. So far the scheme prospers! And yet, this imprudence. . . . If I should fail . . . ? Fail! (*Resolutely.*) To lack courage in a difficulty or ingenuity in a dilemma, are not woman's failings! (*Crosses to table, puts candle on it.* ZEKE *enters* L. 2 E. *carrying a bottle of champagne.* GERTRUDE *crosses* L. *to him. MUSIC stops.*) Well, Zeke? (ZEKE *looks off* L.) Excuse me! *Adolph!*

ZEKE. Dat's right, Missy. I feels just now as if "Adolph" was my legitimate title. Dis here's de stuff to make you feel like a gemman!

GERTRUDE. But is he coming?

ZEKE. He's coming! (*Sound of champagne cork heard off* L.) Do you hear dat, Missy? Don't dat put you all in a froth, and make you feel light as a cork? (*Showing bottle.*) Dere's nothing like the *union brand* to wake up de harmonies ob de heart!

GERTRUDE. Remember to keep watch upon the outside

—do not stir from the spot. When I call you, come in quickly with a light. Now, will you be gone?

ZEKE. I'm off, Missy, like a champagne cork wid de strings cut! Whee! (*Exits* L. 2 E. GERTRUDE *crosses to table. NOISE off* L. GERTRUDE *looks* L.)

GERTRUDE. I think I hear the Count's step! (*Blows out candle. Crosses to* D.R.C.) Now if I can but disguise my voice and make the best of my French.

COUNT. (*Sticks his head in at* L. 2 E., *whispering.*) Millinette! (*Comes on, crosses up to backdrop, feeling his way. MUSIC resumes.*) Millinette, where are you? (*His hand touches the dress-maker's model painted on the backdrop. Bus.*) How am I to see you in the dark?

GERTRUDE. (D.R.C. *imitating* MILLINETTE'S *voice.*) Hush! *Parle bas.*

COUNT. (*Crossing toward her with arms out.*) Come and give me a kiss!

GERTRUDE. Non! Non! (*She ducks under his arm and crosses to* L. *of him.*) Make haste. I must know all!

COUNT. (*Repeats bus.* GERTRUDE *avoids him and crosses to* R.) You did not use to be so deuced particular.

ZEKE. (*Without, over others ad lib.*) No admission, gemman! Box office closed, tickets stopped!

TRUEMAN. (*Without.*) Out of my way! Do you want me to try if your head is as hard as my stick? (*MUSIC up.*)

GERTRUDE. (*Crossing far* D.R., *clasping hands and waving them.*) What shall I do? Ruined! Ruined! (*More ad libs off* L.)

COUNT. Hello! They're coming in here, Millinette! Millinette, why don't you speak? Where can I hide myself? (*Crosses* U.R., *tries to get under painted bed, crosses* L.) Where are all your closets? If I could only get out— or get in somewhere! (*He reaches* U.L.C. *and feels the screen hinged to the drop. Faces front. Loudly.*) Fortune's favorite yet! I'm safe! (*Goes behind screen.*)

(*Enter* MRS. TIFFANY *and* TRUEMAN *followed by*

HOWARD *from* L. 2 E. MRS. TIFFANY *and* TRUEMAN *cross to* R.C. HOWARD *to* D.L. *of table.* PRUDENCE *enters to* D.L.C.)

PRUDENCE. (*Triumphantly.*) Here they are, the Count and Gertrude! I told you so!

(*Enter* ZEKE *with candles* L. 1 E. *The Stage is suddenly brightly illuminated. All see* GERTRUDE *alone and register surprise.*)

TRUEMAN. (*To* PRUDENCE.) And now you see what a lie you have told!

MRS. TIFFANY. Prudence, how dare you create this disturbance in my house? To suspect the Count, too—a nobleman!

HOWARD. (*Crossing* R. *to* GERTRUDE'S L.) My sweet Gertrude, this foolish old woman . . .

PRUDENCE. (*Crossing to* C.) Oh! You needn't talk. I heard her make the appointment. I know he's here! Or he has been here. I wonder if she hasn't hid him away somewhere! (*Circles around* L. *to drop, in step to MUSIC, as* TRUEMAN *speaks.*)

TRUEMAN. (*Crosses to below table, angrily.*) You're what I call a confounded—troublesome—meddling—old —prying— (*On last word, as MUSIC builds,* PRUDENCE *finds the screen and with a grand gesture throws it open, revealing the* COUNT.)

TRUEMAN. (*After a crashing chord from the PIANO.*) Thunder and lightning! (ZEKE *backs to extreme* L. HOWARD *backs up away from* GERTRUDE, *and they ALL stand aghast for an instant.* MRS. TIFFANY *raises her arms in surprise and anger;* HOWARD *looks from the* COUNT *to* GERTRUDE *with an expression of bewildered horror.*)

PRUDENCE. I told you so!

MRS. TIFFANY. (*Crossing* HOWARD *to* GERTRUDE'S L.) You depraved little minx! This is the meaning of your dancing with the Count!

COUNT. (*Crossing down to footlights.*) I don't know what to make of it! Millinette not here! (*Looks* R., *turns front.*) Miss Gertrude! Aha! I see it all,—a disguise! The girl's desperate about me—the way with them all!

TRUEMAN. (*Below table.*) I'm choking—I can't speak! (*Crosses* R. 2.) Gertrude! (*She takes a step toward him, her hands out in desperate appeal.*) No! No! (*He grasps his forehead.*) It must be some horrid mistake! (*Suddenly changes tone.*) The villain! I'll have the truth! (*Crosses toward* COUNT, *threateningly.*) Do you see this stick? You made its acquaintance a few days ago; it's time you were better known to each other. (*He crosses to* R. *of* COUNT *as* MRS. TIFFANY *crosses to centre line.* COUNT *runs around him and gets to* R. *of* MRS. TIFFANY *at* C.)

COUNT. Desist, ruffian! Would you strike a woman? Madam, my dear Madam, keep that barbarous old man off, and I will explain! (*He draws her a step* R.) Madam, with . . . aw . . . your natural *bon gout* . . . aw . . . your fashionable refinement . . . your knowledge of *foreign customs* . . . aw . . .

MRS. TIFFANY. Oh! Count, I hope it ain't a foreign custom for the nobility to shut themselves up in the dark with young women? We think such things dreadful in America.

COUNT. Demme, Madam, I am perfectly innocent in this affair! (*Backs a step.*) I was summoned here *malgré moi*, not knowing whom I was to meet. (*Sternly.*) Miss Gertrude, favor this company by saying whether or not you directed—that . . . aw . . . that colored individual to conduct me here?

GERTRUDE. (*Crossing* L. *to* R. *of* MRS. TIFFANY *as* HOWARD *counters* D.R.) Sir, you well know . . .

COUNT. (*Holding up his hand.*) A simple yes or no will suffice. (GERTRUDE *clasps her hands and crosses down a step, much troubled.*)

GERTRUDE. I . . . I . . .

MRS. TIFFANY. Answer the Count's question instantly, Miss!

GERTRUDE (*Pause.*) Yes, I did. But . . .

COUNT. (*Triumphantly.*) You hear, Madam? (*Crosses to U.L. on R. of* PRUDENCE, *as* MRS. TIFFANY *backs up a step.*)

TRUEMAN. I won't believe it! I can't! (*Crosses L. to* ZEKE.) Here, you, stop rolling your eyes and let us know if she told you to bring that critter here?

ZEKE. (*Very loud.*) I'se refuse to gib evidence; dat's de device ob de skilfullest counsels ob de day! Can't answer, Boss. Neber git a word out ob dis child—Yah! Yah! (*Exit L. 1 E.*)

GERTRUDE. Mrs. Tiffany . . .

MRS. TIFFANY. Paugh! (*Crosses her to L. of* HOWARD D.R.C.)

GERTRUDE. (*Sadly appealing.*) Mr. Trueman, if you will but have patience . . .

TRUEMAN. Patience! (*Crossing in R. to L. of table.*) Oh, Gertrude, you've taken from an old man something better and dearer than his patience. (*MUSIC starts: "Hearts and Flowers."*) The one bright hope of nineteen years of self-denial . . . of nineteen years of . . . (*He staggers to chair L. of table and sinks down in it, weeping, with his head in his hands.*)

MRS. TIFFANY. Get out of my house, you *ow*dacious, (*Crossing to her.*) you ruined . . . you *abimé* young woman. (GERTRUDE *starts to take a step toward her, she withdraws.*) Don't touch me! You will corrupt all my family. Never let me see your face after tomorrow. Pack. (*Crosses up to cloth on R. side.*)

HOWARD. (*Crossing in to R. of* GERTRUDE.) Gertrude, I have striven to find some excuse for you—to doubt— to disbelieve—but this is beyond all endurance. (*Bearing his sorrow with manly pride, he exits R.* GERTRUDE *follows a few steps, her arms out in mute supplication.*)

MILLINETTE. (*Hurrying in at L. 2 E.*) I could not come before . . . (*Stops in surprise at seeing the persons assembled.*) *Mon Dieu!* Vat does ziss mean? (MRS. TIFFANY *crosses to* D.R.C., L. *of* GERTRUDE.)

COUNT. Hold your tongue, you fool! You will ruin

everything. I will explain tomorrow. (*Crosses to* L. *of* MRS. TIFFANY *as* MILLINETTE *crosses up to* L. *of* TRUEMAN.) Mrs. Tiffany, my dear Madam, let me conduct you back to the ball room. (*She takes his arm.*) You see I am quite innocent in this matter. (*They cross toward exit* L. 2 E.) A man of my standing, you know . . . aw . . . you comprehend the whole affair . . . (*Exeunt* L. 2 E.)

MILLINETTE. (*Crossing to* L. 2 E.) I vill say to him von word, I vill! (*Exit* L. 2 E. PRUDENCE *crosses to* L. 2 E.)

GERTRUDE. (*Crossing to below* R. *of table, kneels.*) Mr. Trueman, I beseech you! I insist upon being heard! (*Rises.*) I claim it as a right!

TRUEMAN. (*Rising.*) Right! How dare you have the face, girl, to talk of rights? You had more rights than you thought for, but you have forfeited them all! All right to love, respect, protection, and to not a little else that you don't dream of. (*Gesturing to* R.) Go! (*Pause.*) Go! I'll start for Catteraugus tomorrow. I've seen enough of what fashion can do! (*The events of the last few minutes have aged* TRUEMAN *greatly. He now stumbles toward the exit, a broken man, back bent and tapping feebly with his cane. Exits* L. 2 E.)

PRUDENCE. (*Wiping her eyes,* U.L.C.) Dear old man! How he takes on. I'll go and console him! (*Exits* L. 2 E.)

GERTRUDE. (*At* R.C. *just below chair.*) This is too much! How heavy a penalty has my imprudence cost me! (*Indicating* L.) His esteem, and (*Indicating* R.) that of one even dearer . . . my home . . . my . . . (*MUSIC segues from "Hearts and Flowers" to the lively Polka.* GERTRUDE *listens, crosses* L. *a few steps.*) They are dancing! And I . . . I should be weeping, if pride had not sealed up my tears! (*She raises her head high, marches to chair* R. *of table and sits as:*)

THE CURTAIN FALLS

(MUSIC segues to Intro. of "Why Did They Dig.")

Musical Interlude *following immediately after curtain of Act Four. SELECTION: "Why Did They Dig Ma's Grave So Deep?"—the Ensemble:* MRS. TIFFANY, SERAPHINA, TWINKLE, SNOBSON, MILLINETTE, FOGG, HOWARD,—*or any suitable combination. (Sung in front of Conservatory drop. Tableau arranged in seated and standing positions around low bench.* SNOBSON *seated on floor. The whole to be sung with the utmost seriousness and appreciation for the tender sentiments in the ditty.)*

1st Verse. (Sung as a solo by MRS. TIFFANY.)
Poor little Nelly is weeping tonight,
Thinking of days that were full of delight.
Lonely she sits by the old kitchen grate,
Sighing for Mother . . . but now it's too late.
Under the daisies all covered with snow
Rests the fond Mother away from life's woe.
Nelly is left now to murmur and weep:
"Why did they dig Ma's grave so deep?"
Chorus. (All.)
Why did they dig Ma's grave so deep?
Down in the clay so deep . . .
Why did they leave me here to weep?
Why did they dig Ma's grave so deep?
2nd Verse. (Sung by TWINKLE *with others humming under.)*
Only sweet mem'ries of gladness and love,
Come to the child of the dear ones above,
Shadows are creeping around the lone room,
Early and late there's a feeling of gloom.
Out in the churchyard the wild breezes blow,
Seeming to echo her heart's grief and woe.
Softly she murmurs while chills o'er her creep:
"Why did they dig Ma's grave so deep?"

Chorus. (In harmony.)

3rd Verse. (All. A cappella.)
    Poor little Nelly in slumber's sweet rest,
    Dreams all the night of the Mother so blest;
    Sees her again in a vision of light,
    Praying: "God Bless little Nelly tonight!"
    Smiling upon her with glorified face,
    Calling her home to that bright resting-place.
    Poor little Nelly oft sighs in her sleep:
    "Why did they dig Ma's grave so deep?"

Chorus. (Fortissimo.)

CURTAIN

ACT FIVE

Mrs. Tiffany's *Drawing Room, same as Act One. Chair
at Right. At rise* Gertrude *discovered seated on
ottoman with a writing-pad in her lap and a pen in
her hand.*

Gertrude. (*Troubled.*) How shall I write to them?
What shall I say? (*Puts pad and pen down on her* R.)
Prevaricate I cannot. And yet, if I write the truth—
simple souls! How can they comprehend the motives for
my conduct? Nay! The truly pure and the purely true
see no imaginary evil in others! It is only vice, that re-
flecting its own image, suspects even the innocent. I have
no time to lose . . . I must prepare them for my return.
(*Writes.*) What true pleasure there is in daring to be
frank! (*Writes a few lines more, then pauses.*) Nay! Not
so frank either. There is one name that I cannot mention.
Ah! that he should suspect . . . should despise me.
(*Writes.*)

Trueman. (*Entering* R. *above uppermost wing. Crosses
to* C., *points to* Gertrude *while looking at audience. She,
of course, does not hear him and continues writing
busily.*) Ah! There she is! If this girl's soul had only
been as fair as her face! Yet she dared to speak the truth,
I'll not forget that! A woman who refuses to tell a lie
has one spark of Heaven in her still!

MUSIC CUE: "She's Only a Bird in a Gilded Cage,"
    Mr. Trueman.

She's only a bird in a gilded cage,
A beautiful sight to see.
You may think she's happy and free from care;
She's not, though she'd like to be. (Gertrude *writes
in time with the music.*)
'Tis sad when you think she may waste her life,

80

But youth pays no heed to age.
And her beauty's been sold
For fashion and gold,
She's a bird in a gilded cage.

(*As* TRUEMAN *sings the last lines he crosses slowly toward the* R. *wing, standing half Offstage. Now as he re-enters for the Verse, behind him, close together in a single line and each with a hand on another's shoulder, enter singing* FOGG, HOWARD, TWINKLE, SNOBSON, COUNT *and an unidentified guest not seen before and not to be seen again until the Curtain Call. They walk in step to the music and stop just as the last man in line clears the wing.*)

Verse:
    The ballroom was filled with fashion's throng;
    It shone with a thousand lights,
    And she was a maiden who passed along, (*They turn
        front but face toward* GERTRUDE.)
    The fairest of all the sights.
    A girl to her lover then softly sighed,
    There's riches at her command;
    But she'll marry for wealth, not for love, I cried,
    Just to live in a mansion grand!

Chorus: (*Repeated by the male ensemble, with* GERTRUDE *rising and singing bel canto with them from her place below the ottoman. At an appropriate time they cross* R. *in step and exit into the wings at end of Chorus.* TRUEMAN *remains, and crosses* L. *to* GERTRUDE *who has resumed her seat and her writing.*)

TRUEMAN. What are you writing there, Gertrude? Plotting more mischief, eh girl?
GERTRUDE. I was writing a few lines to some friends in Geneva, New York.
TRUEMAN. (*Crossing down two steps.*) The Wilsons, eh?

GERTRUDE. (*Surprised, rising.*) Are you acquainted with them, Sir?

TRUEMAN. I shouldn't wonder if I was. I suppose you have taken good care not to mention the darkened room —that foreign puppy in the closet—the pleasant surprise —and all that sort of thing, eh? (*Turns* R.)

GERTRUDE. (*With spirit.*) I have no reason for concealment, Sir! for I have done nothing of which I am ashamed!

TRUEMAN. Then I can't say much for your modesty.

GERTRUDE. I should not wish you to say more than I deserve. (*Gets letter from ottoman.*)

TRUEMAN. (*A step* D.R., *aside.*) There's a bold minx!

GERTRUDE. (*Crossing to him.*) Since my affairs seem to have excited your interest . . . I will not say your *curiosity*, perhaps you even feel a desire to inspect my correspondence? There! (*Handing letter.*) I pride myself upon my good nature; you may like to take advantage of it?

TRUEMAN. (*Aside.*) With what an air she carries it off! (*To her.*) Take advantage of it? So I will. (*Takes letter, crosses* D.R.C., *reads it.*) What's this? "French chambermaid — Count — impostor — infatuation — Seraphina — Millinette — disguised myself — expose him!" Thunder and lightning! I see it all! (*Crosses toward her.*) Come and kiss me, girl! (GERTRUDE *evinces surprise.*) No, no, I forgot. . . . It won't do to come to that yet! (*Crosses* R. *a step.*)

GERTRUDE. (*Aside.*) What a remarkable old man!

TRUEMAN. I've found one true woman at last! (*Crosses to her.*) Gertrude, I'll thrash every fellow that dares to say a word against you!

GERTRUDE. (*Crossing to ottoman, sits.*) You will have plenty of employment then, Sir, for I do not know of one just now who would speak in my favor!

TRUEMAN. Not *one*, eh? Why, where's your dear Mr. Twinkle? Oh, I know all about it. Can't say I admire your choice of a husband! But there's no accounting for a girl's taste.

GERTRUDE. Mr. Twinkle! Indeed you are quite mistaken!

TRUEMAN. No . . . really? Then you're not taken with him, eh?

GERTRUDE. Not even with his rhymes.

TRUEMAN. (*Crosses* R. *a step.*) Hang that old mother meddle-much! What a fool she has made of me. (*Crosses to her* R.) And so you're quite free, and I may choose a husband for you myself? Heart-whole, eh?

GERTRUDE. I—I—I trust there is nothing *unsound* about my heart.

TRUEMAN. There it is again! An evasion is a *lie in contemplation!* Out with the truth! Is your heart *free* or not?

GERTRUDE. (*Rising, with great dignity.*) Nay, Sir, since you *demand* an answer, permit *me* to demand by what right you ask the question?

(*Enter* COLONEL HOWARD R. 3 E. *Holds* R.C.)

GERTRUDE. (*Starts, looks at* HOWARD, *then looks at audience, points to him.*) Colonel Howard here!

TRUEMAN. (*Aside.*) I'm out again! What's the Colonel to her? (*Backs Upstage to* R. *of fireplace.*)

HOWARD. (*Crossing to* R. *of* GERTRUDE *who stands* R. *of ottoman.*) I have come, Gertrude, to bid you farewell. Tomorrow I resign my commission and leave this city, (*Crosses up 2 steps.*) Perhaps forever. (*Points accusingly.*) You, Gertrude, it is you who have exiled me! After last evening . . .

TRUEMAN. (*Crossing down to* HOWARD'S R.) What the plague have you got to say about last evening? And what have you to say to that little girl at all? It's Tiffany's precious daughter you're in love with.

HOWARD. Miss Tiffany? Never! I never had the slightest pretension . . .

TRUEMAN. That lying old woman! But I'm glad of it! (*With growing comprehension, as he backs to* R.) Oh! Ah! Um! (*Looking significantly at* GERTRUDE *and then at* HOWARD, *who are gazing deeply at each other.*) I see how it is. So you don't choose to marry Seraphina, eh? (*Step* L.) Well now, whom *do* you choose to marry?

HOWARD. (*Stiffly, crossing* R. *to* R. *of* TRUEMAN.) I shall not marry at all!

TRUEMAN. You won't? Why you don't mean to say that you don't like . . . (*Points to* GERTRUDE.)

GERTRUDE. Mr. Trueman, I may have been wrong to boast of my good nature, but do not you presume too far upon it.

HOWARD. You like frankness, Mr. Trueman, therefore I will speak plainly. I have long cherished a dream from which, last night, I was rudely awakened.

TRUEMAN. Last night you suspected Gertrude of— (*Angrily.*) —of what no man shall ever suspect her of again while I'm above ground! You did her an injustice— it was a mistake! There now, that matter's settled. (*Steps up and indicates* L.) Go, and ask her to forgive you, she's woman enough to do it! Go, go! (GERTRUDE *crosses* D.L. *a step.*)

HOWARD. (*Steps Upstage, facing* TRUEMAN.) Mr. Trueman, you have forgotten to whom you dictate.

TRUEMAN. Then you won't ask her pardon?

HOWARD. Most undoubtedly I will not—not at any man's bidding. I must first know . . .

TRUEMAN. You won't do it? Then if I don't give you a lesson in politeness . . . (*Step to him.*)

HOWARD. (*Bravely.*) It will be because you find me your *tutor* in the same science. I am not a man to brook an insult, Mr. Trueman! But we'll not quarrel in the presence of the lady. (*Crosses* D.R. *a few steps.*)

TRUEMAN. Won't we? I don't know that . . . (*Crosses* R. *a step.*)

GERTRUDE. (*Crossing quickly to* TRUEMAN'S L. *holds him.*) Pray, Mr. Trueman—Colonel Howard! Pray desist, Mr. Trueman, for my sake! Colonel Howard, if you will but read this letter, it will explain everything. (*Hands letter across* TRUEMAN *to* HOWARD, *who takes it and crosses* U.R., *reading.* GERTRUDE *sits on ottoman.*)

TRUEMAN. (*Crossing to her.*) He don't deserve an explanation! Didn't I tell him it was all a mistake? Refuse to beg your pardon! I'll teach him!

HOWARD. (*Turning down, his face lighting up.*) Gertrude! How I have wronged you! (*She rises.*)

TRUEMAN. Oh, you'll beg her pardon now? (*Between them.*)

HOWARD. Hers, Sir, and yours! (*Crosses to her.*) Gertrude, I fear . . .

TRUEMAN. You needn't. She'll forgive you! It's woman's nature to pardon. But come along! I must now find Antony and his wife. I've a story of my own to tell! Come along! Come along! (*They exit* R. 3 E. *Enter* MRS. TIFFANY L. 2 E. *followed by* TIFFANY *who carries a large bundle of bills in his hand.*)

MRS. TIFFANY. (*Crossing to* L. *of Chair.*) I beg you not to mention the subject again. Nothing is more plebeian, nothing more *ungenteel* than looking over and fretting over one's bills!

TIFFANY. (*On her* L.) Then I suppose, my dear, it is quite as ungenteel to *pay* one's bills?

MRS. TIFFANY. Certainly! (*Sits chair.*) I hear the *ee-light* never condescend to do anything of the kind.

TIFFANY. (*Crossing to her* L.) Now listen to what I am going to say. As soon as my daughter marries Mr. Snobson . . .

(*Enter* PRUDENCE L. 3 E. *Runs to* D.L.C. *below ottoman. She waves a three-cornered note in her hand.*)

PRUDENCE. Oh, dear! oh dear! What shall we do!

TIFFANY. What is it?

PRUDENCE. (*Crossing to* C.) Such a misfortune! Such a disaster! (*Crossing* L.) Oh, dear! Oh, dear!

MRS. TIFFANY. (*Rising.*) What *is* the matter?

PRUDENCE. Something shocking, Lizzie! Seraphina's gone!

TIFFANY. (*Crossing* L. 2 *steps.*) Gone? Where?

PRUDENCE. (*Crossing to him.*) Off! Eloped! Eloped

with the Count! (*Crossing* R. *to* R. *of* MRS. TIFFANY.)
Dear me, dear me! I always told you she would!

TIFFANY. (*Sinking down on the ottoman.*) Then I am
ruined!

MRS. TIFFANY. Oh, what a ridiculous girl! And she
might have had such a splendid wedding! (*Crosses up
to fireplace at back.*)

TIFFANY. (*Jumps up, crosses to* PRUDENCE *at* D.R.C.)
Prudence, are you *sure* they are gone?

PRUDENCE. Just look at this note—one might know
by the very fold of it . . .

TIFFANY. (*Snatching it.*) Let me see it! (*Crosses* L.
as he reads it, to R. *of ottoman, as* MRS. TIFFANY *crosses
down a step.*) "My dear Ma, when you receive this I
shall be a *countess!* Isn't it a sweet title? The Count and
I were forced to be married privately, for reasons which
I will explain in my next. You must pacify Pa, and put
him into a good humor before I come back, though now
I'm to be a countess I suppose I shouldn't care!" Un-
dutiful huzzy! "We are going on a little excursion and
will be back in a week. Your dutiful daughter—Seraphina." A man's curse is sure to spring up at his own
hearth. Here is mine! The sole curb upon that villain
gone, I am wholly in his power! (*Staggers toward chair
R.*) Oh! The first downward step from honor . . . he
who takes it cannot pause in his mad descent, and is
sure to be hurried on to ruin! (*Sits.*)

MRS. TIFFANY. (U.C.) Why, Mr. Tiffany, how you do
take on!

(*Enter* TRUEMAN, L. 3 E. *followed by* GERTRUDE *and*
HOWARD. *He crosses to* L. *of* TIFFANY. GERTRUDE
and HOWARD *hold* D.L.C.)

TRUEMAN. Where are all the folks? Here, Antony, you
are the man I want. Why—what's the matter? There's
a face for a thriving city-merchant! (*Lifting him from
chair.*) Ah! Antony, you never wore such a hang-dog
look as that when you trotted about the country with

your pack upon your back! Your shoulders are no broader now— (*Glancing at* MRS. TIFFANY.) but they've a heavier load to carry, that's plain.

MRS. TIFFANY. (*Crossing to* R. *of ottoman.*) Mr. Trueman, such allusions are highly improper! What would my daughter, *the Countess,* say?

GERTRUDE. The Countess? Oh! Madam!

MRS. TIFFANY. (*Crossing toward her.*) Yes, the Countess! No wonder you're surprised after your *recherché, abimé* conduct! You are dismissed, do you understand? Discharged! (*Sits* R. *side ottoman.*)

TRUEMAN. (*Crosses* 1 *step to her.*) Have you done? Very well, it's my turn now. (*MUSIC starts: "Hearts and Flowers."*) Antony, perhaps what I have to say don't concern you as much as some others—but I want you to listen to me. You remember, Antony, a blue-eyed smiling girl . . .

TIFFANY. Your daughter, Sir? I remember her well.

TRUEMAN. None ever saw her to forget her! Give me your hand, man. There—that will do! Now let me go on. (*He takes a position* U.C.) I never coveted wealth, yet twenty years ago I found myself the richest farmer in Catteraugus. This cursed money made my girl the object of speculation. Every idle fellow that wanted to feather his nest was sure to come courting Ruth. There was one . . . my heart misgave me the instant I laid eyes upon him . . . for he was a city chap, and not overfond of the truth. But Ruth . . . ah! . . . (*Crosses to* TIFFANY.) she was too pure herself to look for guile! His fine words and fair looks . . . the old story. Then one morning the rascal robbed me—not of my money, he would have been welcome to that—but of the only treasure I cherished . . . (*Step* L.) my daughter!

TIFFANY. But you forgave her!

TRUEMAN. (*Turning down.*) I did! But a year after they were married he forsook her! She came back to her old home—her old father! It couldn't last long! She pined—and pined—and pined—and then she died! Don't think me an old fool, though I am one . . . for grieving won't bring her back. (*Weeping, he turns up and leans an elbow on the fireplace.*)

TIFFANY. (*Rising.*) It was a heavy loss!

TRUEMAN. (*Turning to him and speaking so loudly that* TIFFANY *falls back into the chair.*) So heavy, that I should not have cared how soon I followed her, but for the child she left! As I pressed that child in my arms, I swore that my unlucky wealth should never curse it, as it had cursed its mother! It was all I had to love—but I sent it away—and the neighbors thought it was dead. The little girl was brought up tenderly but humbly by my wife's relatives in Geneva, New York. (GERTRUDE *looks front, wide-eyed.*) I had her taught true independence. She had hands, capacities, and she learned to use them! Money should never buy her a husband! for I resolved not to claim her until she had made her choice, and had found the man who was willing to take her for herself alone. She turned out a rare girl! and it's time her old grandfather claimed her. Here he is to do it! (*Crosses down one step.*) And there stands Ruth's child! Old Adam's heiress! Gertrude! Gertrude! My grandchild! (GERTRUDE *rushes into his arms* C., MRS. TIFFANY *rises to* L. *of ottoman. MUSIC stops.*)

PRUDENCE. (*To* R. *of chair.*) Do tell! I want to know! But I knew it! I always said Gertrude would turn out to be somebody after all!

MRS. TIFFANY. Dear me! Gertrude an heiress! (*Crosses* R. *to her.*) My dear Gertrude, I always thought you a very charming girl . . . quite *you-nick*—an heiress! (*Crosses* R. *to* PRUDENCE.) I must give her a ball! I'll introduce her to society myself. An heiress must make a sensation!

HOWARD. (*Extreme* L.) I am too bewildered even to wish her joy. Ah! there will be plenty to do that now—but the gulf between us is wider than ever.

TRUEMAN. Step forward, young man, and let us know what you are muttering about. (*Crosses to* HOWARD.) I said I would never claim her until she had found a man who would love her for herself alone. I think I have found that man! And here he is! (*Strikes* HOWARD *on the back.*) Gertrude's yours! There, never say a word, man; don't bore me with your thanks—you can cancel all obligations by making that child happy! (*He hands her to* L.) There! Take her! Well, girl, what do you say?

GERTRUDE. (*On* HOWARD'S R.) That I rejoice too much at having found a parent for my first act to be one of disobedience! (*Gives her hand to* HOWARD.)

TRUEMAN. How very dutiful! (*Crossing to* C.) And how very disinterested! (TIFFANY *crosses* U.C.; MRS. TIFFANY *crosses to up of chair.*)

PRUDENCE. (*To* TRUEMAN.) All the *single folks* are getting married!

TRUEMAN. No they're not. You and I are single folks, and we're not likely to get married. (*Crosses to* R. *of ottoman.*)

MRS. TIFFANY. (*Now very sweet, crossing* L. *to* TRUEMAN.) My dear Mr. Trueman—my sweet Gertrude, when my daughter the Countess returns, she will be delighted to hear of this *deenooment!* (*Crosses and sits chair* R.C.)

GERTRUDE. The Countess? (*Crossing to* MRS. TIFFANY.) Pray, Madam, where is Seraphina?

MRS. TIFFANY. At this moment on her way to . . . to . . . Washington! Where, after visiting all the fashionable curiosities of the day, including the President, she will return to grace her native city!

GERTRUDE. But, Madam, Seraphina is not married!

MRS. TIFFANY. Excuse me, my dear, but this morning my daughter had the honor of being united to the Count *dee Jolly-may-ter.*

GERTRUDE. (*Backing upstage a step.*) But, Madam, he is an impostor! (TIFFANY *cross to above ottoman.*)

MRS. TIFFANY. Good gracious, Gertrude! How disrespectful thus to talk of a man of rank! An heiress, my dear, should have better manners! The Count . . .

MILLINETTE. (*Enters* L. 3 E., *crying, crosses to* R. *of* TRUEMAN *at centre line.*) Oh! Madame! I veel tell everyzing—oh! zat *monstre!* He break my heart!

MRS. TIFFANY. (*Rising to* R. *of chair.*) Millinette, what is the matter?

MILLINETTE. Oh, zat man, ze Count, he promise to marry me! I love heem so much! And now Zeke say he run away wiz Mademoiselle Seraphina! (*Consternation. All ad lib.*)

MRS. TIFFANY. What insolence! The girl is mad! (*Crossing* R. *to* L. *of* PRUDENCE.) Count *Jolly-may-ter* marry my *femmy de chamber!*

MILLINETTE. (*Crossing to* L. *of chair.*) Oh! Madame, he eez not one Count, not at all! Zat eez only ze title he go by in zees country. Ze foreigners always take zee large title ven zey do come here. His name *à Paris* vas Gustave Tread-mill. But he not one Frenchman at all. He just live long time in Paris. (*Counting on her fingers.*) First he leev weez Monsieur Vermicelli—zere he was ze head *cook!* Zen he leev vid Monsieur Tire-nez, ze barber! After zat he leev vid Monsieur le Comte Frippon-fin— and dere he vas ze Count's *valet!* Zere! Now I tell everyt'ing I feel one great deal better! (*Sits chair and crosses her legs.*)

MRS. TIFFANY. Oh! good gracious! I shall faint! (*Crosses to* R. *of* PRUDENCE, D.R.)

(*Enter* SNOBSON L. 3 E. *to below ottoman, as* TIFFANY *crosses around ottoman to come down on his* L. HOWARD *crosses further* D.L.)

SNOBSON. (*Evidently a little intoxicated.*) I won't stand it! I say I won't!

TIFFANY. (*Holding his* L. *arm.*) Mr. Snobson, for heaven's sake . . .

SNOBSON. Keep off! I'm a hard customer to get the better of. You'll see if I don't come out strong! (MIL-LINETTE *rises and crosses to up of chair next to* GER-TRUDE.)

TRUEMAN. Where are your manners, man?

SNOBSON. (*Crossing to* TRUEMAN *at* C.) My business ain't with you, Catteraugus; you've waked up the wrong passenger! (*Aside.*) Now, the way I'll put it into Tiff will be a caution. I'll make him wince! That extra mint julep has put the true pluck in me. Now for it! (*Crosses to* TIFFANY.) Mr. Tiffany, Sir—you needn't think to come over me, Sir—you'll have to get up a leetle earlier in the morning before you do *that,* Sir! I'd like to know, Sir, how you came to assist your daughter in running away with that foreign loafer? It was a downright swindle, Sir. After the conversation I and you had on that subject she wasn't your property, Sir.

TRUEMAN. (*Down a step.*) What, Antony, is that the way your city clerk bullies his boss?

SNOBSON. (*A step* R.) You're drunk, Catteraugus! Taken a leetle too much toddy, my old boy! Be quiet! (*Aside.*) Now to put the screws to Tiff! (*Crosses* L.) Mr. Tiffany, Sir . . . you have broken your word, as no virtuous ind-i-vid-ual, no honorable member of . . . the . . . comm-un-i-ty—

TIFFANY. (*Aside to him.*) Have pity, Mr. Snobson, I beseech you! I had nothing to do with my daughter's elopement! I will agree to anything you desire . . . your salary shall be doubled . . . trebled . . .

SNOBSON. (*Aloud.*) No you don't. No bribery and corruption!

TIFFANY. (*Aside.*) I implore you to be silent. Do not speak . . . you are not yourself at this moment.

SNOBSON. (*Loudly.*) Ain't I though. I feel *twice* myself. I feel like two Snobsons rolled into one, and I'm chock full of the spunk of a dozen! Now, Mr. Tiffany, Sir . . .

TIFFANY. I shall go distracted!

TRUEMAN. (*Crossing close to* SNOBSON.) Turn him out, Antony!

SNOBSON. He daren't do it! Ain't I up to him? Ain't he in my power? Can't I knock him into a cocked hat with a word? (*With growing violence.*) And now he's got my steam up—I will do it! (*Crosses to* C.)

TIFFANY. (*In place.*) Mr. Snobson . . . my friend . . . !

SNOBSON. It's no go—steam's up—and I don't stand at anything!

TRUEMAN. (*Crossing* 1 *step* R.) You won't *stand* here long unless you mend your manners. You're not the first man I've upset because he didn't know his place!

SNOBSON. I know where Tiff's place is . . . and that's in the *State's Prison!* He's a *forger,* Sir! (TIFFANY *throws himself onto the ottoman in an attitude of despair; the others stand transfixed with astonishment.*) He's been forging Dick Anderson's endorsements of his notes these ten months. He's got a couple in the bank that will send him to the wall anyhow, if he can't make a raise. I took them there myself! Now you know what he's worth. I said I'd expose him and now I have done it! (*Crosses* R. *and sits chair, as* MILLINETTE *and* GERTRUDE *withdraw a step up and* HOWARD *crosses up to* L. *of ottoman.*)

MRS. TIFFANY. (*Crossing* PRUDENCE *to* R. *of* SNOBSON.) Get out of my house! You ugly, drunken brute, get out!. (*Crosses to* TRUEMAN.) Mr. Trueman, you have got a stick, put him out!

(*Enter* SERAPHINA L. 2 E. *to* D.L.C. *She wears her bonnet.*)

SERAPHINA. (*To front.*) I hope Zeke hasn't delivered my note.

MRS. TIFFANY. (*Crossing* D.C.) Oh, here is the Countess!

TIFFANY. (*Starting from his seat, crosses to her* R. *Seizes her violently by the arm.*) Are—you—married?

SERAPHINA. Goodness, Pa, how you frighten me! No, I'm not married, *quite.*

TIFFANY. Thank Heaven!

MRS. TIFFANY. (*Crossing* L. *to* R. *of* TIFFANY.) What's the matter? Why did you come back?

SERAPHINA. The clergyman wasn't at home. I came back for my jewels. The Count said that the nobility could not get on without them. (*She crosses* L. *a step or*

two as HOWARD *crosses above ottoman to join* GERTRUDE
U.R.C.)

TIFFANY. (*Crossing* L. *a step.*) I may be saved yet!
Seraphina, my child, you will not see me disgraced—
ruined! I have been a kind father to you—or I've tried
to be one—although your mother's extravagance made
a *madman* of me! (*On the word he runs his hand over
his head from back to front disarranging his hair, and
steps toward* MRS. TIFFANY, *who utters a cry of fright
and sinks down on the ottoman.*) The Count is an
impostor! (SERAPHINA *reacts. He crosses to* C., L. *of*
TRUEMAN *who has edged a step* R.) You seemed to like
him. (*Pointing to* SNOBSON.) Heaven forgive me! Marry
him and save *me.* Mr. Trueman, as my oldest friend, will
you advance the sum which I require—I pledge myself
to return it. (*Crossing* L. *to* R. *of* SERAPHINA.) My wife,
my child . . . who will support them when I'm in . . .
the thought makes me frantic! You will aid me? You had
a child yourself.

TRUEMAN. But I did not *sell* her. Shame on you,
Antony! To put a price on your own flesh and blood!
Shame on such foul traffic!

GERTRUDE. (*Crossing to him at* C.) Mr. Trueman . . .
Grandfather, I should say—save him—do not embitter
our happiness by permitting this calamity to fall upon
another . . .

TRUEMAN. Enough. I did not need your voice, child.
I am going to settle this matter in my own way. (*Crosses
to* SNOBSON, *pulls him out of the chair and across to his*
L.; *as* GERTRUDE *crosses to* U.R. *of ottoman.*)

SNOBSON. (*Waking up.*) Eh? Where's the fire? Oh, it's
you, Catteraugus.

TRUEMAN. If I comprehend aright, you have for some
time been aware of your principal's forgeries? (*As he
says this, he beckons to* HOWARD *who crosses to* R. *of
chair as witness.* MILLINETTE *counters to* R.)

SNOBSON. You've hit the nail, Catteraugus! Old chap
saw I was on to him six months ago; left off throwing
dust into my eyes . . .

TRUEMAN. Oh, he did?

SNOBSON. Made no bones of forging Anderson's name at my elbow.

TRUEMAN. Forged at your elbow? You saw him do it?

SNOBSON. I did!

TRUEMAN. Repeatedly?

SNOBSON. Re-pea-ted-ly!

TRUEMAN. Then, you rattlesnake, if he goes to the State's Prison, you'll go with him. You are an accomplice, an *accessory!* (TRUEMAN *sits chair.* HOWARD *meets* GERTRUDE *up of chair.* SERAPHINA *by* L. 1 E.)

SNOBSON. (U.C.) The deuce, so I am! I never thought of that! Must make myself scarce. I'll be off! (*Crosses to* TIFFANY'S R. *at* L. *of ottoman.*) Tiff, I say, Tiff, that drunken old rip has got us in his power. Let's give him the slip and be off. They want men of genius in the West —we're sure to get on! You—you can set up as a writing-master and teach copying *signatures;* and I—I'll give lectures on *temperance!* (TIFFANY *crosses* L.) You won't come, eh? Then I'm off without you. Good-bye, Cat-teraugus! Which is the way to California? (*Exits* L. 3 E.)

TRUEMAN. (*Rising and crossing to* C.) There's one debt your city owes me. Now let us see what other nuisances we can abate. Antony, I shall not say much about what you have done. Your face speaks for itself,— the crime has brought its punishment along with it.

TIFFANY. (*Crossing* R. *to* TRUEMAN'S L.) Indeed it has, Sir! In *one year* I have lived a *century* of misery.

TRUEMAN. I believe you, and I will assist you, upon one condition.

TIFFANY. My first, my kindest friend, only name it!

TRUEMAN. You must sell this house and all its gew-gaws, and bundle your wife and daughter off to the country. (MRS. TIFFANY *rises and crosses* D.L. *to* SERA-PHINA.) There let them learn economy, true independ-ence, and home virtues instead of foreign follies. As for yourself, continue in your business, but let moderation in future be your counsellor, and let *honesty* be your confidential clerk.

TIFFANY. Mr. Trueman, you have made existence once more precious to me. (*Crossing* D.L.C.) My wife and daughter shall quit this city tomorrow, and . . .

PRUDENCE. (*Crossing to below chair as* MILLINETTE *crosses* D.R.) It's all coming right! We'll go to the county of Catteraugus tomorrow!

TRUEMAN. No, you won't. I make that a stipulation, Antony; keep clear of Catteraugus. None of your fashionable examples there! (TIFFANY *crosses to* R. *of* MRS. TIFFANY; PRUDENCE *to* R. *of chair.*)

(JOLIMAITRE *appears from behind* R. *of ottoman, having entered* L. 3 E., *holding a cloak up to his face.*)

COUNT. (*Aside.*) What can have detained Seraphina? We must be off!

MILLINETTE. (*Perceiving him, crosses to his* R. *as* TRUEMAN *edges up and to the* R. *a little.*) Here he is! Ah, Gustave, mon cher Gustave! I have you now and we never part no more. Don't frown, Gustave, don't frown . . .

TRUEMAN. (*Stepping down on* R. *of* MILLINETTE.) Come forward, Mr. Count! and for the edification of fashionable society confess that you're an impostor.

COUNT. Impostor! Why you abominable old . . .

TRUEMAN. Oh, your feminine friend has told us everything, the cook, the valet, the barber, and all that sort of thing. Come, confess, and something may be done for you.

COUNT. (*With a shrug.*) Well then, I do confess I am no Count; but really, ladies and gentlemen, I may recommend myself as a most capital cook!

MRS. TIFFANY. Oh, Seraphina!

SERAPHINA. Oh, Ma! (*They retire up.*)

TRUEMAN. Promise me to call upon the whole circle of your fashionable acquaintances with your own advertisements and in your cook's attire, and I will set you up in business tomorrow. Better turn stomachs than turn heads!

COUNT. I accept with pleasure! (TRUEMAN *crosses to* GERTRUDE.)

MILLINETTE. (*On his* R.) But you will marry me? (MRS. TIFFANY *and* SERAPHINA *cross down* L.)

COUNT. Give us your hand, Millinette! Sir, command me for the most delicate *paté*—the daintiest *croquette à la royale*—the most transcendent *omelette soufflée* that ever issued from a French pastry-cook's oven. (*To the* TIFFANYS.) I hope you will pardon my conduct, but I heard that in America, where you pay homage to titles while pretending to scorn them, where *Fashion* makes the basest coin current— (*Turns* R.) where you have no kings, no princes, no *nobility* . . .

TRUEMAN. (*Coming forward to* C.) Stop there! (*MUSIC CUE: "Columbia the Gem of the Ocean."*) I object to your use of that word. When justice is found only among lawyers, health among physicians, and patriotism among politicians, *then* may you say that there is no *nobility* where there are no titles! But here in these United States of America we *do* have kings, princes, and nobles in abundance—but they are of *Nature's* stamp, if not of *Fashion's!* And we do have honest men (*Indicating* HOWARD, *who stands at attention.*) warm-hearted and brave. And— (*Indicating* GERTRUDE.) we do have women, gentle, fair, and true . . . to whom no *title* could add *nobility!* (*MUSIC up. From above is lowered a cut-out of an American eagle, with flags, and below it the motto, "Nobility Forever."*)

CURTAIN

OTHER TITLES AVAILABLE FROM SAMUEL FRENCH

CAPTIVE
Jan Buttram

Comedy / 2m, 1f / Interior

A hilarious take on a father/daughter relationship, this off beat comedy combines foreign intrigue with down home philosophy. Sally Pound flees a bad marriage in New York and arrives at her parent's home in Texas hoping to borrow money from her brother to pay a debt to gangsters incurred by her husband. Her elderly parents are supposed to be vacationing in Israel, but she is greeted with a shotgun aimed by her irascible father who has been left home because of a minor car accident and is not at all happy to see her. When a news report indicates that Sally's mother may have been taken captive in the Middle East, Sally's hard-nosed brother insists that she keep father home until they receive definite word, and only then will he loan Sally the money. Sally fails to keep father in the dark, and he plans a rescue while she finds she is increasingly unable to skirt the painful truths of her life. The ornery father and his loveable but slightly-dysfunctional daughter come to a meeting of hearts and minds and solve both their problems.

OTHER TITLES AVAILABLE FROM SAMUEL FRENCH

COCKEYED
William Missouri Downs

Comedy / 3m, 1f / Unit Set

Phil, an average nice guy, is madly in love with the beautiful Sophia. The only problem is that she's unaware of his existence. He tries to introduce himself but she looks right through him. When Phil discovers Sophia has a glass eye, he thinks that might be the problem, but soon realizes that she really can't see him. Perhaps he is caught in a philosophical hyperspace or dualistic reality or perhaps beautiful women are just unaware of nice guys. Armed only with a B.A. in philosophy, Phil sets out to prove his existence and win Sophia's heart. This fast moving farce is the winner of the HotCity Theatre's GreenHouse New Play Festival. The St. Louis Post-Dispatch called Cockeyed a clever romantic comedy, Talkin' Broadway called it "hilarious," while Playback Magazine said that it was "fresh and invigorating."

Winner!
of the HotCity Theatre GreenHouse New Play Festival

"Rocking with laughter...hilarious...polished and engaging work draws heavily on the age-old conventions of farce: improbable situations, exaggerated characters, amazing coincidences, absurd misunderstandings, people hiding in closets and barely missing each other as they run in and out of doors...full of comic momentum as Cockeyed hurtles toward its conclusion."
–Talkin' Broadway